HAUNTED LAKE TOMAHAWK

MEMOIRS OF A GHOST HUNTER

HAUNTED LAKE TOMAHAWK

MEMOIRS OF A GHOST HUNTER

MARK PALBICKI

Henschel
HAUS
publishing, inc.
www.henschelHAUSbooks.com

MILWAUKEE, WISCONSIN

Published by
HenschelHAUS Publishing, Inc.
www.henschelHAUSbooks.com
Milwaukee, Wisconsin

ISBN: 978159598-943-7
LCCN: 2022952131

Printed in the United States of America

Table of Contents

PREFACE

Haunted Lake Tomahawk: Memoirs of a Ghost Hunter is a personal journey of one man exploring the possibilities of existence after death. Come join the fun, and excitement, as the author recounts local ghost stories shared by residents of Lake Tomahawk, Wisconsin, the surrounding area, and other strange Northwood's anomalies.

More than just stories, Mark takes you along on exciting investigations of actual ghost hunts, at local places, with known paranormal activities. You'll even get to know some of the ghosts, as the author describes them in life and also shares personal paranormal experiences with you.

AUTHOR'S NOTE

The paranormal stories you are about to read are firsthand accounts of events as told by the people of Lake Tomahawk and the surrounding areas. Their stories are for you, the readers, to judge for yourselves. It is up to you to decide if you believe in them or not.

The paranormal research investigations are real. The people and places are real. I have tried to take an nonjudgmental stand on them. But I do take these stories at face value.

With that being said, I confess I believe there's more than meets the eye to the world we live in. I truly hope you enjoy this book as much as I did researching and writing it!

WELCOME TO HAUNTED LAKE TOMAHAWK

MEMOIRS OF A GHOST HUNTER

*This book is best if read
with an open mind.*

ACKNOWLEDGMENTS

First and foremost, I would like to thank the people of Lake Tomahawk for sharing their ghost stories with me. Without them there could be no book.

Secondly, I would like to thank my paranormal research team, which I fondly dubbed "Fulcrum" (both as a nickname—and for good reason)! Members varied from hardcore skeptics, to true believers, from scientific minds to spiritual hearts. It was always a balancing act (to say the least) when they would come together, hence the name Fulcrum. A special shout-out to these guys for putting up with me and all of my craziness.

Members of Fulcrum:
     Jeff Braun
     Pat Barney
     Scot Mortier
     Br. Rodd Umlauf

Special thanks go to Mr. Andrew Sommers, graphic artist, who is a truly talented craftsman. Andrew took my pencil sketch designs and worked his magic on them. The cover, the back of this book, as well as some illustrations, are examples of his artistic genius. Somehow he managed to reach inside my mind to get the exact results I was looking for. I can't recommend him highly enough. If you agree, he can be reached at: metalacide@yahoo.com

For Judy Loose, my editor and formatter, all I can say is thank you for not giving up on me. You left this world too soon, but even after your passing, you had the foresight to save my work, allowing team member Scot Mortier to step in and finish the process. Rest peacefully, Judy.

To Tom Cattani, filmmaker and long-time friend, who stepped in as the book neared completion to provide his skills in video editing and documenting one of the team's investigations.

Finally, daughters Megan and Katelyn, thank you both for some great ideas and suggestions you presented, and help with proofreading.

Lastly, but not least, to my lovely wife, Donna, for her endless support, understanding, and freedom that allowed me to expand my thinking, grow as a person, and accomplish my goal of publishing this book.

In the end, the evidence speaks for itself, but also to each of us personally, as it is to be understood according to our individual gifts and life experiences.

Mark Palbicki

THE TOWN

Lake Tomahawk Snow Hawk

OUR TOWN

Lake Tomahawk is widely proclaimed as "The Snowshoe Baseball Capital of the World" with good reason: this town has put a different twist on America's favorite pastime. You can't miss the welcoming signs, on both ends of town, proclaiming just that. A league has been established, so that during summer, on about any given Monday night, this quiet little town opens itself to some friendly ball-playing rivalry. As advertised, the game is played on snowshoes, something you don't see every day, making it all the more unique and interesting, and Lake Tomahawk a *destination*, if you will.

The town really comes together for these games, which are more than just ordinary. They are events the town takes great pride in hosting.

The concession stand next to the ball field is operated by many local organizational groups, a different volunteer group taking the reins for each game. This camaraderie of cooperation helps strengthen the community's well-being and identity.

As a plus, there is always a special game played on the 4th of July. Our hometown team, the Snow Hawks, usually plays against their southern rival, the Chicago All-Stars, on that day. Thousands of spectators descend upon our little town; it absolutely comes alive.

Adorning Main Street are American flags, and if you listen closely, you can hear them flapping in the summer breeze as they set the stage in applause for the annual 4th of July parade. There is a decorative float competition where local establishments compete for bragging rights and a traveling trophy for display in their shop's window. And candy, lots and lots of candy, tossed skyward from the parade participants to waiting kids who line up four to five deep along the parade route in anticipation of a tasty treat.

Following the parade is the snowshoe baseball game. Watch out for the melon ball! (They use real melons!) Afterwards, the town puts on some of the best fireworks the Northwoods have to offer.

This holiday is Smalltown, USA, and is really about as Americana as America can get!

Personally, there is no other place I'd rather be, on Independence Day than in Lake Tomahawk.

Oh, one last thing, lest I forget—the freshly baked pies! Often, there are more than fifty different varieties on hand, mostly homemade, all delicious, and willingly donated by volunteers.

Makes me want to sing *"Oh, Danny boy, the pies, the pies are calling,"* but instead I say, "Come for the game and stay for the pies!" (Or is it, "Come for the pies and stay for the game?")

LAKE TOMAHAWK —THE WAY LIFE SHOULD BE

I t was once put to me that, "If the sitcom *Cheers* was in a town, it would be Lake Tomahawk."

Mind you, it's not exactly a picturesque little town that's been cut out of a storybook, but it does, by its own right, have a certain amount of charm and character all on its own.

It is surrounded by the natural beauty of the Northern Highland American Legion State Forest, with seemingly endless trails for hiking, biking, and motorized sports, all to explore.

This is where the rivers run gin-clear and the lakes abound.

Seems like there is always something to do, be it a lazy afternoon tube ride down the Wisconsin River or tangling with a mighty musky. This area has plenty of opportunities for sportsmen and nature lovers alike. It is truly one of Wisconsin's hidden gems and best-kept secrets!

I've heard, "In the dead of winter up here one could run butt naked through the middle of downtown and nobody would notice!" (I'm pretty sure I was sitting in one of the local establishments when I first heard this one.)

Our town is about as close as it gets to a real-life version of the TV series, *Northern Exposure.* It is just chock full of hearty characters, from one end of town to the other! I find their endearing qualities to be the fabric of which the town is woven.

It is here, within that tapestry, that our story begins to take shape, one strand at a time, as the people of Lake Tomahawk gracefully share their personal paranormal experiences with us.

The stories you are about to read are first-hand accounts of events that took place. The paranormal investigations are real, the people are all real. You must determine for yourself whether or not you want to believe their stories. I am nonjudgmental on these issues, and take them for their face value.

THE CABIN

HOW I CAME TO BE IN LAKE TOMAHAWK

D o you believe in *serendipity* or *synchronicity?* I've learned when coincidences happen that seem to be more than just a coincidence, pay close attention, because they happened for a reason.

Coincidences are the Universe's way of reaching out to you, and letting you know something. These omniscient moments may be clear as crystal, or take a round-about way of getting your attention, depending on how you learned to read them.

What if I told you that a beer bottle opener is what brought me to Lake Toma-hawk? Would you think that sounds crazy?

Grandpa Casey's beverage of choice:
Fox Head.

It was a Fox Head 400 beer can opener, to be exact.

I had just started a new position as a model maker in the International Model Shop at Briggs and Stratton Corporation. I had been on the job for about a week when I was approached by an engine tech and asked to do a favor. He produced a beer bottle opener from his pocket and asked if I could polish it for him.

"No problem," I replied.

He said he had a busy morning and that he'd be back to pick it up in the afternoon.

"Before you go, what's your name?" I asked.

"It's Mike," he said, matter of factly.

"Hi Mike, I'm Mark."

I treated the buffing wheel with some rubbing compound and proceeded to polish the opener. It didn't take but a few minutes to clean it up nicely. Mike returned that afternoon, flagged me down, and I gave him the brightly polished opener.

"What do I owe you?" Mike questioned.

"Nothing. Might I ask, where'd you get it from?"

"I've got an old cigar box full of them," he offered.

"Really? Are there any *Fox Head Beer* ones?"

"Why *Fox Head*?" he asked.

"I save them because that was my grandpa's favorite beer. It's my way of remembering him."

"I'll check when I get back home tonight," Mike said.

The next morning, Mike produced a *Fox Head* opener and gave it to me.

Now I was the one asking how much I owed.

"Nothing. My grandma passed away and we're cleaning out her old cabin up north. We're going to be putting it up for sale," he said.

Now I was curious. "Whereabouts up north?"

"Lake Tomahawk," he told me.

It's hard to believe that happened over 25 years ago. I'll never forget our first impressions of our future cabin. As my wife Donna simply put it, "It's an eyesore." The back door had rotted off its hinges, and its current occupants were a family of skunks. It probably would have been proper to put a match to it. Synchronicity told me to look beyond the cabin's dilapidated state.

The more I thought about it, the more I believed I had been guided to this cabin by my departed grandfather, Casey. Could finding it actually be a gift from him? It's really kind of hard to put into words, but an overwhelming sensation came over me that day, a feeling like I already belonged. That feeling remains in me to this day.

The old cabin on Dorothy Lake

GHOST STORIES & LOCAL HAUNTS

OUR OWN AMITYVILLE

This story starts at the Lake Tomahawk Meat Market.

"You have to get there early or they'll all be gone," my wife, Donna, said.

So off to the meat market I went. One of Lake Tomahawk's many secrets are Todd's fresh-baked turnovers. Only offered on Sunday mornings, they are out of this world! I got there a bit too early. Todd told me that they were still in the oven and to come back in about half an hour.

I told him, "Save me three."

"What kind?"

"Apple."

When I came back, my timing was perfect. The turnovers had just come out of the oven, still hot, but not too hot to eat.

"Here you go," Todd said as he handed me the white paper sack. "Anything else I can do for you?"

"Nope! Not unless you have any good ghost stories to tell me."

Todd lit up like a pinball machine and told me, "Go see Melinda, the bartender at Smiley's. She lives in the Amityville Horror house."

"The Amityville Horror house?"

"Yea, it's the most haunted house in town."

"Where is it?"

"On the south end of town where Highway D meets 47."

I thanked Todd and with my sack of apple turnovers grasped in my hand, went on my merry way.

Owners Melinda and Nicklaus Cleveland, originally from Hazelhurst, Wisconsin, recently purchased the old gambrel-roofed house where Hwy D and Hwy 47 meet in a T-intersection. I'm pretty sure the house got tagged with the name because of the barn-like shape of its roof. It does bear an eerie resemblance to the Amityville Horror House.

"It was the perfect project house and we got it really cheap," Melinda told me.

"So, Melinda, what makes you think your house is haunted?"

Melinda's Story

"Well, it all started when we decided to renovate the upstairs bedrooms. We had rented out one of those big Dumpsters. The first experience was in one of the bedrooms where we found a really old green blanket, kind of pea green, must have been from the

1950s or '60s. We started gutting the room out—walls, ceiling, floor—everything, including that blanket. Everything went into that Dumpster. Well three days later, that green blanket shows up back in the same bedroom."

She continued, "So I'm like, 'Nicklaus, you better not be messing with me!'"

She went on to explain. "The only reason I said that was because, just after we had purchased the house, I was at the BP gas station here in town when a woman approached me, a complete stranger to me at the time, and asked if we had bought the old place. To which I responded yes.

Then she tells me, 'You know it's haunted, don't you?'

I will admit that did play on my mind a bit.

"So, anyway, getting back to what I was saying, Nicklaus responded about the blanket being back by saying, 'No, I wouldn't do that to you.'"

That's when I asked him, "Could you please get rid of it," and back to the Dumpster it went.

"Well, three days later, that damned green blanket is back and I'm scared shitless! Finally we drove the blanket to the Oneida County Landfill, never to be seen again," she said.

She then mentioned more had happened.

"The second occurrence was in the bathroom. We had washed all the walls and had given them a fresh coat of white paint. When we returned the next day, we discovered what I would only describe as a child's scribbling or drawing in crayon on our freshly painted walls. Now, our kids are older, and well, way beyond that stage. Plus the fact that we don't even have any crayons in the house. Not a single one."

As I continued to listen, she went on.

"The latest thing that happened occurred on the basement staircase. Nicolas cut his foot open really badly on a big huge triangular-shaped piece of lead that was on one of the basement steps. We recently had a cement floor poured down there, and went up and down those steps at least a thousand times. There was nothing on them, period!"

#

I spoke to Nicklaus next.

Nicklaus told me there are times when their dog Hank will stare and bark at a corner of the living room for no apparent reason.

He also conveyed to me that the upstairs bedrooms had locks on the outside of the doors.

My gut reaction was that there had been some kind of child abuse, or unwarranted imprisonment, going on in that house in the past.

While interviewing Melinda, she told me to go back and talk to Todd, who might have something to add.

So next time I saw Todd, I let him know about my contact with Melinda, and that she indeed had some stories to tell. "She also said that I should talk to you."

"I already told you," Todd replied.

"Nope, you said something about Rhinelander but never went into any details."

Lake Tomahawk's own "Amityville Horror House." Notice the similarity

Todd's Story

"That's something else," Todd said, "but I did use to date a girl who lived in Melinda's house."

"She told me that she heard some commotion coming from the far upstairs bedroom like stuff was getting tossed around the room, so she went to investigate."

Todd continued.

"The noise grew louder as she approached the room. When she opened the door, there was complete silence, like a void from any sound. However, the whole room was in disarray. Every drawer from the dresser has been opened and their contexts emptied onto the floor. Clothes from the closet were no longer hanging on their hangers. Toys were thrown all over the place. There was a boxed puzzle that was opened and all the pieces were scattered about. Yet, there was nobody in there to do this!"

I listened intently.

"She went to go get her mom, to tell her what had happened. They both returned to the room. Mind you, only a short few minutes had transpired. As they opened the door, they discovered that the room was spotless, and everything was in perfect order." No explanation of what happened was ever revealed.

Todd did finally share his Rhinelander story.

"It was back in my younger years. I was living in this old house; it was over 100 years old back then. It was so old that it had a stable out back for horses instead of a garage for a car.

"Well, one day, I had a few buddies over. We were all in the living room when we heard a knock on the door. We all heard it—three knocks.

"I shouted, 'Door's open, come on in,' expecting it to be our last buddy arriving.

"You could hear the door open and close and the shuffling of feet. Our heads turned to greet our friend as he turned around the corner of the hallway to enter the living room. But there was nobody there. I even got up to look. Nobody!

"A short time later, our buddy arrived, and we asked him, 'Were you just here, and forgot something and went back out?'

"No," he replied. "I just got here."

"Back then, we didn't think too much about it. We were pretty hungover from the night before. But looking back, we know it happened."

"Sounds like a residual ghost," I told him.

"It's about the energy," Todd responded. "It can't be created or destroyed, it just changes form."

"Yes! Albert Einstein," I said, recognizing one of his many famous quotes.

ONE FINAL GIFT FOR NANCY

When I first approached Dan Dosemagen, Nancy's husband, to ask him if he had any ghost stories he'd like to share for this book, he gave me a half-crazed look and scoffed at the idea.

A resounding, "NO," was his answer.

"I don't have any ghost stories," he said, with a hint of sarcasm in his voice.

But, within a few short minutes, he must have warmed up to the idea and started telling me all kinds of spooky stories revolving around his deceased father-in-law, Rollie.

Dan's Stories

"After Rollie's death," Dan said, "Nancy and I had to go to his residence and get the place ready to go up for sale at auction. This included cleaning."

"One of my duties was to sweep out the 3-car garage. We had struck a deal with the auction company that would allow them to set up and try to sell some of their own antiques out in the garage. Well, the day before the auction company was to come, I swept that garage floor clean from corner to corner, every square inch of it.

He paused, then told me, "Anyways, first thing the next morning, when I un-locked the door and entered the garage, I noticed, there lying on the floor (—now get this—) in the very exact spot where we found Rollies' body lying dead, was a 50-cent piece.

"Now, I know I had swept every square inch of that floor the day before, and I'm here to tell you, that that 50-cent piece wasn't there when we left. It just wasn't there! The hair on the back of my neck stood straight up. Can you guess why? Guess who collected 50-cent pieces? Rollie's daughter, Nancy."

"Wow!" I commented. "It may very well of been one final present from Nancy's dad."

Dan continued. "Then there was the house. This was during wintertime and we

The garage where Dan found the 50-cent piece.

were constantly going in and out of the place. The house wasn't very well insulated, so what Rollie used to do was keep the doors open on any cabinets that were attached to the outside wall, especially under the kitchen sink, so the pipes wouldn't freeze."

"Being somewhat anal," Dan said, "I distinctly remembered closing all those doors before we left for the evening, only to return the next day to discover they'd all be wide open."

Dan stared right at me and said, "Now, you tell me, there are no such things as ghosts!"

Dan didn't stop there.

"There's one final story. Rollie owned a Mercury Sable, which we inherited after his death. Well, Nancy's daughter needed a car, so we gave it to her.

"For some reason, that car kept locking its doors. She knew, with certainty, that she left the doors unlocked, only to return to a locked vehicle. This happened on several occasions. There were also noises coming from the back end of the car. Nancy's daughter couldn't find the source of the noise. She even took it in to the mechanics a couple of times and they found nothing."

Dan paused, then told me, "Finally, the door lock thing happened again while one of the grandkids was in the car, and the kid said "GRANDPA! STOP IT! YOU'RE SCARING US!" and after that, it never happened again. IT NEVER HAPPENED AGAIN!"

HAVE POLTERGEIST, WILL TRAVEL

I Call Him "Wenzel"

Our next ghost story just goes to show that you never know where the next narrative will come from. This tale came to my attention quite unexpectedly, 650 miles away from Lake Tomahawk in the Bluegrass state of Kentucky.

On our annual trek to Florida, my wife Donna and I decided to make a stop to pay a visit to Vicki Hiedeman, an old friend of ours. She lived in Louisville, but had once owned a trailer on Lake Tomahawk's North Avenue, a couple doors down from the Bible Church on Rainbow Road.

We arranged a visit, including a night out for dinner and drinks, followed by a stay at Vicki's condo. It had been a while since we'd seen Vicki, so there was a lot of catching up to do. While the ladies were busy doing that, I went and ordered refreshments. Returning to the table, I apologized for taking so long.

"No need to apologize," Vicki chimed in, then asked, "So, Mark, what have you been up to lately?"

I was a little hesitant on how to answer. We've known Vicki for some time, and that she took her convictions to Christianity quite seriously. Would she be offended or condemning? My mind volleyed back and forth as to how she would react.

I decided to roll the dice and let the chips fall where they may. I told her I was in the middle of writing a book.

"Oh, really? What's it about?"

"Ghosts, ghost stories, investigations, cryptozoology, paranormal stuff. I'm going to title it *Haunted Lake Tomahawk*."

"You're kidding?" Vicki said, with a quizzical expression crossing her face.

"No, not kidding," I replied, matter-of-factly.

"You know what? I may have a story for you."

"It has to be about Lake Tomahawk, or be Lake Tomahawk-related."

"It is," she promised.

I told her I was all ears and began to listen.

"Do you remember my old neighbor, Ellie, up there?" she asked.

"Yes, I remember Ellie. I remember her very well."

"Ellie told me about some strange things going on in her trailer after her husband Wenzel had passed away."

Now she really had my attention.

"What type of strange things are you talking about?" I asked.

"Well, Ellie had this bookshelf in her living room where she proudly displayed her knickknacks. Over the years, her husband Wenzel and family members liked to buy her little figurines for special occasions. She just loved them. She would often reminisce when she looked at them, and could tell you the backdrop story on each figurine. They brought back precious memories to her." Vicki paused, staring off into the distance as she remembered Ellie.

"Anyway, Ellie told me after Wenzel passed away, the figurines would somehow

Photo of actual bookshelf where poltergeist
activity took place.

go about rearranging themselves. They would move from one place to another, seemingly all by themselves.

She continued, "Ellie said she knew exactly where she left them, that she lived there all by herself, that there was nobody else. Somehow by morning, some of her figurines would be shuffled around into different places. There was even a time or two where a piece would go missing, only to turn up on a different shelf altogether.

Ellie wondered how that was possible.'"

"Stuff moving around by itself sounds like poltergeist to me," I said.

Wenzel loved to fish on Dorothy Lake.

I never got a chance to interview Ellie about this; she had long since joined her beloved husband Wenzel in eternal rest. However, I did get the chance to interview their son Rainer, who now owns the property.

The Interview

I had heard from one of my neighbors, Carl Konyn, that Rainer was in town, so I made it a point to stop on over for a visit. I knocked on Rainer's glass patio door and noticed some movement on the inside. I thought, "Good, he's home."

Rainer answered the door and I reintroduced myself, "It's been a few years since we last met."

"Yes, I remember you," Rainer said. "You were one of my dad's friends."

"And your mom's."

"How can I help you?"

"What I'm about to tell you is going to sound a little strange to you but you probably already know about it," I said.

"Know about what?"

"I have a story to tell you about your mother."

"I'm listening."

I repeated the story Vicky had told me down in Louisville, about the poltergeist activity that his mother had experienced.

"No, this is the first time I'm hearing of it." From Rainer's demeanor, he seemed taken aback by Vicki's story. He took a half-step back, looked me straight in the eyes, and said, "After the passing of my father, I had similar experiences."

"Really?"

"Only it was back at my residence in Dayton, Ohio. It got to the point where I thought that somebody was getting into my house at night and moving stuff around," he said, almost in disbelief.

Now I was the one taken a bit aback.

I asked Rainer for permission to do a paranormal investigation at his trailer, to which he agreed.

Everything I had ever read, studied, or heard about poltergeist activity is that there usually is a central catalyst connected to the activity. Remove said agent, and the activity stops. In just about every case, the catalyst is usually an emotionally charged individual. This was obviously not the case here, which left me scratching my head.

Question to the reader: When we die, is it possible for our energy to be dispersed into different fragments, or be dispersed into different places and times, possibly even being in multiple places at the same time?

Original site of Old Army Pete's cabin on the
corner of Rainbow and Lilly streets.

OLD ARMY PETE

From what I could gather, back in his day, Peter Iverson was known to be quite a character and a bit of a spitfire. What he lacked in physical size, he more than made up for with his larger-than-life persona and no-nonsense stature. Pete was known to show up at town hall meetings dressed in his World War II Army uniform and carrying his trusty rifle, especially when he had a bone to pick with the town board members. Here are a couple of short stories about his cabin.

#

While working on Pete's cabin, carpenter Mike Chevalier told me that he had a visitor that made the hair on the back of his neck stand straight up. He said he could *sense* the presence of Old Army Pete.

Mike also said he could *smell* the distinct odor of *Bigger Hare* brand chewing tobacco, which was Pete's favorite brand of chew.

"I knew Pete in life," Mike added, "and we spent a lot of time together. I could recognize the smell of his chew anywhere. I'm telling you, it was Old Army Pete alright."

This occurred during a deck build and partial renovation after the cabin was moved to its current Dorothy Lake location.

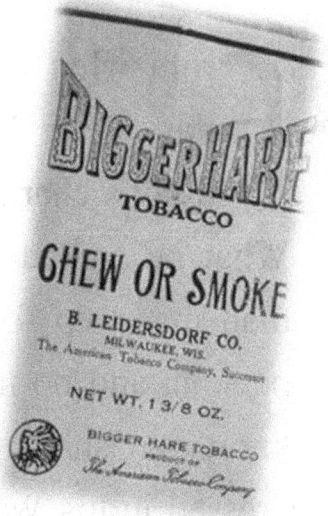

Dona Kloes, proprietor of the Village Café, always looked out her kitchen window while doing dishes. From her vantage point, she could see Old Army Pete's cabin—before we moved it.

Dona swears that on several occasions, a crow landed on Pete's front door, as if trying to open it. Yes, you read that correctly: a *crow* would land on the front door of the old cabin as if it were trying to get in. She said this happened more than just a few times, and, for a while, it was a daily occurrence. This prompted me to buy a crow decoy from Jeff and Jeanie Smith, over at J&J's Sports, and attach it to Army Pete's front door. Then I paid Dona a visit at the diner, just to have a little fun.

"Oh, look! I didn't believe you," I piped up. "There's a crow on the cabin's door."

She came running to take a look, and stood next to me, staring out the kitchen window. It didn't take Dona long to realize the prank. I was promptly greeted with a slap to the back of the head.

"Very funny, ha-ha. I don't care if you believe me or not, but I'm telling you the crow does land there."

"How can it even be possible, when the door is vertical?" I asked.

She responded, "I don't know; it just does!"

The more I thought about it, she was probably right. Crows have talons to hold on with.

At one time, crows were associated with being bad luck omens, or even a symbol of impending death. Alfred Hitchcock's movie *The Birds* features these fine feathered friends, and a flock of crows is called a *murder*.

Nowadays, they get a much better rap, including how smart and clever they are.

They are even smart enough to differentiate human faces. So yes, they can recognize you.

All I could figure out is that on Old Army Pete's door, there are three small windows. Perhaps the crow was attracted to its own reflection?

It was mentioned to me in passing that perhaps the crow was actually Old Army Pete himself reincarnated.

Current location on Dorothy Lake.

LIKE FINE
SEASONING

I could not write a book about the paranormal in Lake Tomahawk without mentioning the Kloes family. To me, the surname of Kloes is synonymous with the word "paranormal." As you read this book, you will find their names and their stories are peppered throughout, scattered like a fine seasoning, either through first-hand accounts, local hauntings, or tall-taled ghost stories.

The Kloes family may very well be the most experienced residents in town when it comes down to paranormal activity.

The most recent activities were at the Village Cafè, and Eric and Jessica Kloes' private residence, where the paranormal activity is ongoing, as of this writing. At these sites, fuses blow, fans turn on by themselves, and electrical breakers trip without any reason.

A couple of months ago, Jessica told me, "I redecorated our bathroom with signs that have biblical quotes on them. For some reason, the same two signs have been falling off the wall. It will be like, in the middle of the night, when all is still, then BAM! It's loud enough to wake the whole

The signs that wouldn't stay put

family. I tried several times and different ways to reattach the signs to the wall but to no avail. It seems that at least once a week, those two signs would fall and crash to the ground."

"Why?" she wondered. "And why only those two signs? I think it's my mom's way of reminding us…" she trailed off.

Jessica finally gave up trying to hang those signs and instead placed them on a ledge where they remain to this day.

She continued, "Then one day our daughter Victoria, Dona's first grandchild, had her cell phone fly off the kitchen table all by itself. To this day, we still have no explanation to how this actually occurred.

"Victoria was only 1½ years old when Dona passed away but you could tell there was a very special bond between them. Also, the other night when we were working late on the café remodel, I was down in

Eric and Jessica Kloes' residence.

the basement. I got overcome by an eerie feeling that I was not alone. I could feel Dona's presence."

All of this activity prompted me to ask Jessica and Eric for permission to do one last paranormal investigation at the Village Café, to which they happily agreed.

WHEN THE OLD HAG COMES CALLING

While visiting the old cabin on Dorothy Lake, long-time friend Candase Price experienced an episode of what is known as sleep paralysis or the "Old Hag Syndrome." During our interview, Candy reported, "I couldn't breathe. It was like there was a suffocating weight on top of my chest, and it kept getting heavier and heavier. I became paralyzed somehow. I finally managed to let out a scream, which snapped me out of it."

Here's my wife Donna's account of what happened that morning. "I was suddenly awakened by a blood-curdling scream, which instantly put me into a fight-or-flight mode. I thought maybe that a bear or something had broken into the cabin and was attacking our friend DeeDee, who was sleeping on the couch.

"My gaze turned to DeeDee to see if she was okay. She had also been awakened by the scream. We glanced around the cabin to find Candy sitting in the upright position in the upper berth of one of the bunk beds, shaking like a leaf."

"Are you okay?" I asked.

My wife Donna and friend Candy.

"What the hell just happened?" Candy blurted. "I couldn't breathe—it was like someone was sitting on top of me!"

#

This is another story I personally relate to. Twice, I have experienced the *Old Hag*.

First, let me try to explain what sleep paralysis is. By definition: sleep paralysis is a brief loss of muscle control known as atonia, which occurs just after falling asleep or just before waking up. It can be brought on by sleep deprivation or lack of sleep.

On to my first experience.

Donna and I were visiting a family I'll call the "Smiths," who had just moved from Chicago to Wisconsin and were in the midst of turning their new house into a home.

Mr. Smith greeted me as I walked into the box-filled living room and was quick to offer me a cold brew.

"Yeah, that sounds good. It's a hot one out there today," I began the conversation.

"I sure could use one too," Smith responded

"How's the settling-in process going? Looks like you guys have your work cut out for you."

"Well, I experienced a panic attack last night," Smith stated.

"Really? What happened?"

Smith went on to describe in full detail what he had gone through.

"I don't think you had a panic attack," I said after listening to his story. "It sounds more like the *Old Hag* paid you a visit," I chuckled.

"The what?" Smith queried.

"The *Old Hag*," I said. "I learned about that kind of stuff in a paranormal class I took at a community college. Its technical name is *sleep paralysis*.

Smith said, "Never heard of it, but it scared the crap out of me."

"I believe you. We just studied it. I never personally experienced it myself," I said, taking a swig from my beer.

Later that evening, back at home, our old central air conditioner was having a hard time trying to keep the house cool. The heat had persisted all day and into the evening. Our master bedroom, located upstairs, made the air a good five degrees hotter.

That night, I could not get comfortable. I tossed and turned until finally deciding to head to a downstairs bedroom, where it would be cooler. I hadn't been down there for more than a half hour when I felt Donna crawl into bed next to me.

She decided she wanted to snuggle. A warm feeling came over me and I smiled. Suddenly, her weight on top of me was starting to get heavy, really heavy. My mind shifted from pleasure to *survival mode* as the weight increased.

I tried to slip off the bed sideways, only to discover that I couldn't move, no matter how hard I tried. The weight became suffocating as I desperately tried to escape the paralyzed state I was in.

Finally, I managed to open my eyes and, just like that, the experience was over. Nobody was there! Donna had never been in the bed.

I did give Mr. Smith a call later that day to sarcastically thank him.

"Remember that *girlfriend* of yours you were telling me about from the other night? Well, thanks a lot! That *Old Hag* decided to follow me home." To this, we both laughed.

The second occurrence happened in Florida, but this time around, my mind recognized what was happening and I knew how to beat her.

So, if you ever find yourself in such a situation, all you have to do is JUST OPEN YOUR EYES .

THE HOUSE ON TOP
OF THE HILL

"**M**ark Wilson lives on the top of the hill in the white house. You really need to talk with him. He's Ann Kloes' grandson and I'm sure he has some good stories for you," reported Dan Dosemagen.

"I felt Ann's presence up there on the hill on more than one occasion," chimed Kathy Mitchell.

I'm the type of person who likes to follow leads wherever they may take me. Ann Kloes' name has been brought to my attention on several occasions now. I've even written about some of Ann's antics in her younger years, in Carol Elwin's, the ghost train story. I must admit, that by now I was becoming somewhat intrigued by just the name of Ann Kloes, and what awaited me on top of the hill in the white house.

Ann was the matriarch of the Kloes family. What good ghost stories she must have had or been involved in. I've tried on a few occasions in the past to contact her grandson, Mark Wilson, via Messenger but to no avail. It was time to try again.

I was in the middle of a plumbing job at the cabin, and, as it goes, the trips to the hardware store average three times when it comes to plumbing. It was on my second trip when on a whim, I decided to drive by Mark's place. Perhaps it was Ann who crossed my mind?

"Hey, I'm in luck," I thought. "Looks like somebody's home."

So up the hill I went.

In the backyard was a guy with a garden hose. He was spraying down the back of the apron of his driveway and waved for me to stop where I was.

I rolled down my window and asked if he was Mark Wilson.

"Don't come any closer!"

Oh, oh, maybe he's unapproachable. He wouldn't be the first.

"Just park where you're at. I don't want to splash any paint on your truck. I had some company over last night and a gallon of paint accidentally got knocked over and I'm washing it down."

"Are you Mark Wilson?" I asked again.

"Yes, I am."

"Good, I've been trying to get ahold of you about my *Haunted Lake Tomahawk* book project."

"Oh, yeah, I saw your message."

"Do you have any good ghost stories about your grandma that you'd like to share? According to some of the locals, she might be haunting this place or something," I said.

Mark chuckled. "Nope, sorry. Nothing like that."

"Okay, sorry to have bothered you." My shoulders slumped as my expectations for a good story rapidly deflated.

As I turned to return to my truck, Mark called after me. "The only thing I know that was haunted around here is the house next to the flea market on the south end of town. The one with the gambrel roof."

Well, that stopped me dead in my tracks. I spun around 180 degrees and faced Mark again.

"Oh, the Amityville Horror House," I chuckled.

"And from what I've gathered, it still is," I said. "But maybe you can enlighten me some. There seem to be some missing pieces of information that the current owners are still unaware of."

"Like when was it built?" I asked.

"Oh, I'd say sometime in the late 1950s."

"Do you know by whom?"

"Sure. It was built by my great-uncle Gust Kloes. Tommy and Sheri Zinda were the original owners."

"Tommy Zinda, Tommy Zinda. Boy, that name sure does ring a bell for me. Maybe from my fishing club days."

"Well, he did own a couple of bait shops over in Minocqua," Mark replied.

"That's it! That's where I know him from. His nickname was Toad or something? No, that's not it."

"It was Tadpole. We used to call him Tadpole Tommy."

"Haven't seen him in forever. Wonder how he's doing nowadays," I said.

Mark said, "He passed away around 10 years ago or so."

"Oh, sorry to hear that. He was always a friendly guy."

"A bit too friendly at times. We used to call him 'the milkman'."

"My great-uncle Gust used reclaimed lumber they got from two or three old buildings that were being razed in the Tomahawk area. One of the buildings used to be an old whorehouse."

"Now, that's interesting."

"That's what they figured caused the haunting to begin with. It was the reclaimed lumber," Mark added.

"Well, that's enlightening. I never would've guessed that I actually knew the guy who once owned that place. From my knowledge base, from what I've read or heard, a lot of hauntings are connected with remodeling projects. Here you have the whole house. You've answered some unanswered questions I had about that place. Thanks for your time, Mark."

"Oh, wait. There's one other thing about that house that might interest you."

"What's that?" I asked.

"An exorcism was performed on the house itself."

"Are you shitting me?"

"No, the pastor from the Bible Church at the time performed it," Mark added.

"Is that the church on Rainbow Road by the tree in the middle of the road?"

"That's the one."

"Do you remember the year?"

Mark scratched his head. "I'd say around 1979 or 1980."

"That's very enlightening indeed!" My juices were now flowing. "It was nice meeting you. Glad I stopped."

"Stop by anytime. I usually have coffee going," Mark said, smiling.

"Thanks. I just may do that."

My mind raced after our conversation. I needed to talk with the good deacon, Rodd Umlauf.

As I made the turn on Rainbow Road past his residence, I spotted Rodd working out in one of his gardens. I swiftly made a right turn into his driveway and rolled down my window.

"Hey, Rodd."

"Hey, Mark."

"You're never going to believe what I just found out." In my excitement, I didn't allow Rodd to respond. "Remember the Amityville Horror House story?"

Rodd nodded.

"Well I finally got to talk with Mark Wilson, and he told me that Tadpole Tommy was the guy who originally owned it."

"I know Tadpole," Rodd said, as he reminisced about a past glory. "I won a musky tournament that he was sponsoring some years back." A smile appeared on Rodd's face.

"That's not all." I continued. "Did you know an exorcism was performed on the place, back around 1979 or 1980?"

This caused Rodd to pause from his work and a shocked look appeared on his face as he shook his head 'no' in disbelief.

I continued, "It was performed by the local pastor of the Bible Church here in town. Do you by any chance know who that pastor might've been back then?"

Rodd looked up from his gardening. "What was that timeframe again?"

"I think 1979 or 1980."

Rodd paused for a minute or two, in deep thought.

"Yes. Yes, I remember who the pastor was, and I think you may know him too."

"Really? Who is it?" At that point, I was about ready to burst with anticipation.

"Do you remember my friend Douglas Crow? We all went out for a fish fry with him."

"Yes. Are you telling me Douglas Crow was pastor at that time?"

"He was, but that was a long time ago."

So Douglas Crow might be the exorcist, I thought. One more lead to follow.

Now I needed to interview Crow about this matter and, in the back of my mind, I couldn't help wonder what other secrets the house on top of the hill holds.

The Exorcist

(continuation of
"House on the Top of the Hill)

So Douglas Crow might be the exorcist...

"So you're saying that Douglas Crow might have been the exorcist? That's the first time I'm hearing this," Br. Rodd Umlauf said, a surprised look on his face.

"He went by a different name back then. I don't know about the exorcism but, if memory serves me correctly, he was the pastor of the church during that time period you're looking for."

I thanked Rodd for the information. Piecing this story together had required some detective work and a history lesson on the town of Lake Tomahawk.

I had only met Doug Crow a couple of times, but it had been one of his stories that first inspired me to write this book. (See *Beloved Zoe* in the *Pet Cemetery* chapter.) I still wasn't sure if there was any truth to the story that he was the exorcist.

How to approach Doug, on this subject matter played on my mind for a while. Would he be receptive to an interview or not? There was only one way to find out. I knocked on his door and asked him.

It was an interesting interview with Douglas Crow. He told me how he began his journey as a man of the cloth, cutting his teeth as a prison chaplain. He then became a minister at the Bible Church in Lake Tomahawk. While pastor of the church, Doug was asked to perform an exorcism on the house of Shirley Zinda and her two daughters, ages twelve and fourteen at the time.

Here is Douglas Crow in his own words:

"They sought out help at our church because they were hearing and seeing things that were terrifying them," Douglas told me. "They came to me because they were scared—they believed that something was going on within the house itself."

Doug paused, gathering his thoughts, then continued, "I wasn't even sure if it really happened. I didn't sense anything out of the normal as I went through every room in the house."

He told me that on the walk-through, he invoked God, repeatedly saying, "In the name of Jesus Christ, I command you to leave this house and don't come back."

"I did it all. This took just over an hour. You know, I went by faith. I believed in exorcisms. The Zindas lived there for a few more years and, as far as I know, the exorcism was a success. They were happy with the results, so I was happy. They said it never came back."

Doug was surprised by the news that the paranormal activity had started up again. After all, over 40 years had gone by since the exorcism.

"It sounds like the recent remodeling project brought the activity back," I said.

It hadn't occurred to me that something as simple as a remodeling could restart a haunting.

Doug sighed.

There is one other thing the new home-owner, Nicklaus Cleveland, had told me.

"He said that the upstairs bedrooms had the locks on the doors *facing the hallway,* rather than having locks inside the room."

"Why would someone do that?" Doug asked."

"That sounds like possible abuse," I surmised. Doug nodded in agreement.

Doug then said, "You know, locking somebody in there like that, that could invite some unwanted things. Who knows? There was no doubt in my mind that the Zindas believed what was going on in that house was real."

"You know what, Doug," I confessed. "A couple of times now, I've had things follow me home after investigations, harmless for the most part. We pretty much suspect who the entity is, but it did manage to put a good scare into my wife Donna."

"I, too, have had a lot of weird things happen over the years—unexplainable things. I don't even try to explain them anymore," Doug replied.

"Yeah, sure seems like there's a lot more to this world than meets the eye."

"Quantum entanglement for one," Doug added.

"Yeah, that's some spooky stuff," I said.

"You know, I believe we live in a spiritual world."

A long pause.

"Well, it was nice talking with you, Mark."

With that our interview ended.

*Disclaimer:

While I can't stop wondering about the reversed locks on the bedroom doors—who were they for and what purpose did they serve—the reporting of this curiosity is not intended to accuse anybody of wrongdoing. All I know for sure is that's the condition in which the new owners found the house.

HAUNTED PUBS

SPOOK CENTRAL

Slo's Pub

10599 Big Arbor Vitae Drive
Woodruff, WI 54568

Greg and Sue Slominski are owners of this
ever-popular bar located on Big Arbor Vitae
Lake in Woodruff, Wisconsin.

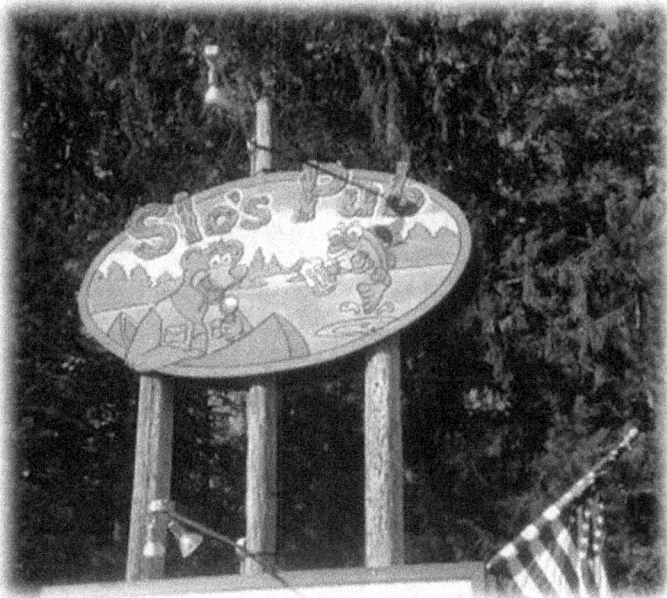

Interview with
Sue Slominski

"It was in our early days up here, just after purchasing the tavern, Greg was still working for the phone company, or 'Ma Bell' as he likes to put it, and he was still in transit between our Germantown residence and here at our tavern in Arbor Vitae. So it was just me and our son Jordan, who was about 10 years old at the time, staying above the bar while Greg was away at work."

Sue said she could hear the main entrance door of the bar opening and closing all night long. "I'm not kidding you! I'd come down all by myself in the middle of the night in my nightgown to check the door to make sure it was locked and secured. Looking back, I don't know what I was thinking. What would've happened if it had been a robber or something? But, every night, this would happen. It was driving me crazy! I lost close to 45 pounds in 3 months because I couldn't sleep.

"I did catch wind that at one time, this place used to be a brothel! This makes me wonder sometimes ... maybe that … I don't know, maybe that's what really is behind all that commotion at the front door."

I answered, "Over the years with what I've experienced of the paranormal, anything's possible. It could very well have something to do with it."

So, readers, could the paranormal activity at the front door possibly be tied to the spirits of long-departed johns, just looking for a little late-night company?

"Wait, there's more," Sue said with a devilish twinkle in her eye. "You might want to shut off the tape recorder for this one," she added.

"On the weekends when Greg came home, and it would be as if different disembodied ladies of the evening took turns using my body to pleasure my husband. The experience was incredible!"

A slight blush fell upon Sue's face. (As Greg smiled and nodded in total agreement.)

"Perhaps a succubus was at play," I surmised.

"I don't care what anyone tries to tell me," Sue continued, "I will never deny that the front door opened and shut all by itself. It got to the point where I couldn't even sleep at night. I'd be up at 3:00 or 4:00 in the morning, put on a pot of coffee, and start working on painting the ladies' room. It really got that crazy!"

Owner Greg Slominski poses with the Irma
UFO up on Herman's Hill

Interview with Kyle Hunter, Bartender

Weird Beard

Kyle Hunter is a seasoned bartender who has been working at Slo's Pub for the past six years.

"It was around closing time, I had already locked the main entrance door and went back behind the bar to count the till. The cash register is located facing the outdoor seating area overlooking the lake. That's when it first happened.

"I looked up, out the window towards the lake. I saw an unfamiliar face reflected in the glass. The guy was sitting at the table directly behind me. When I turned to tell him that the bar was closed, he was gone! I turned back around, thinking my eyes had played a trick on me and continued counting the day's till.

"When I looked up again for the second time, there in the reflection was the same old man again! But this time, I paused and got a really good look at him. He had a long white beard, probably close to two feet in length."

I interrupted Kyle for a second and chuckled, "ZZ Top!"

Kyle smiled back and continued, "I'd say he was in his sixties or seventies, a real old-timer. His clothing was not of this era, not even this decade, maybe from the 1940s or something. Strange thing is, he was only visible from the waist up. It was like he had no bottom half.

"Once again, I turned around, certain of what I just saw, and once again he was gone! A bit unnerved now, I returned to counting the register. I couldn't help but look up for a third time, but this time when I looked into the reflection, he was gone. I never saw him again."

I asked Kyle if there were any other stories he'd like to share.

"Well, yes. Yes, there are," Kyle replied matter-of-factly. "While stocking down in the basement after bar closing, I swear I could hear people walking around up here, in the bar area. This has happened on more than one occasion.

"I'd come up to investigate, only to find no one here. Another time, a stuffed toy dog that was perched on top of the hot chocolate machine seemed to get tossed off while I was looking directly at it!

"Still another time while heading downstairs through the kitchen area, I saw just the bottom half of a person walking past the stairwell in the basement."

I kidded around with Kyle, asking him if it was the bottom half of the apparition he had seen in the reflection in his earlier story.

He replied, "No, this one was wearing more modern-style blue jeans and tennis shoes. but like I said, it was only the bottom half. There was nothing from the waist up!"

At this point, Greg chimed in and added that one morning, he went into the basement and discovered a case of beer had been smashed all over the floor. He questioned Kyle as to why it wasn't cleaned up the night before.

Kyle replied that the basement was clean and in order when he left. This prompted Greg to look through security footage, only to see that the case of beer seemingly threw itself off the stack.

Kyle's last words to me were, "Though I witnessed several weird experiences at Slo's throughout the years, never once did I feel threatened."

#

My initiative at Slo's Pub was to collect some ghost stories and do a little investigating of my own. I had found earlier that another paranormal investigation team named "The Breezer Files" had conducted an investigation. Check out this husband-and-wife paranormal team on YouTube: https://www.youtube.com/watch?v=NjS_imq_AXA.

Our investigation in the basement was short. We noticed that a good majority of our instruments were going off. Our EMF devices were pegging and our thermal imaginer had whole walls that were all aglow, at which time our electrical engineer team member Pat Barney sounded, "We are in the midst of an 'electrical storm' down here, gentlemen!"

With that, we had seen enough. Our instruments would be rendered useless under these conditions.

Through my endless studies of the paranormal, I acknowledge that there is a train of thought out there that's been going around for quite some time, which believes ghosts/spirits/aberrations are drawn to electrical energy. If this is true, one could say that Slo's Pub might certainly be considered a beacon for such activities.

One could conclude that the electrical storm we experienced may very well be the reason for the amount of paranormal activity that takes place there. For this reason, I've nicknamed Slo's Pub "Spook Central." (Or perhaps they might be in need to get a good electrician?)

Special Beer Delivery

I stopped in town for gas at the BP, looked up, and saw Jeanne Godar at the next pump filling her tank as well. I remembered talking to her a few years back about hospice patients and their stories while sipping a few cold ones over at Smiley's Sports Bar.

I shot her a quick wave and asked her if she had any good ghost stories she would like to contribute to my book.

"No, not really, but the person I think you should talk to would be Judy Peardon."

Some years back, Judy Peardon and her ex-husband owned the Gas Light Tavern on the north end of town.

When I interviewed Judy, she claimed that a mischievous entity, who went by the name of Frank, would playfully tug at her hair, and that she wasn't alone.

"He liked girls. I wasn't the only one," she said.

Judy's lips curled into a smile, as she adjusted herself in her chair. "I'd be working behind the bar and catch him out of the corner of my eye. He'd be walking in front of the kitchen area, then when I'd turn to look, he'd be gone. "

"You could also hear him as he'd walk on the steps leading to the upstairs apartments. It was a distinct sound; there was no mistaking it. Then, when you'd go to take a look, of course, no one would be there," she continued.

"Actually, come to think of it, he came with the place. If you don't believe me, just ask the previous owners, and they'll tell you."

I told her I might just do that.

"So, Judy, I'm curious about how you know who the ghost is. I noted that you called him by the name of Frank. Now how would you know that?"

"Well, back in the day, we used to play with a OUIJA board upstairs. One time, we asked the board who was haunting the place and the board spelled out his name, F….R…A….N…..K, Frank.

"But the planchette didn't stop there. It also spelled out his occupation. At one time, he used to deliver beer here. From then on, we just called the ghost Frank, the beer delivery guy."

I took Judy's advice and contacted the sons of previous owners, the Stentz brothers, who had grown up in the tavern.

Apparently, according to Tim Stentz, years ago, when the tavern was called Mac and Mins, an actual shooting took place on the premises. Tim couldn't remember the fellow's name or if the guy died on the premises or not. "Probably not," Tim added.

Bitters and Bulls Bar/Restaurant.

Judy returned to the tavern, which is now called "Bitters and Bulls," a couple of years ago as a cook. She said that the building has gone through several remodels and additions. She hasn't experienced anything out of the norm. She didn't feel that Frank resides there any more.

Lady in White

Barb Elhers and her husband Dan own the Shamrock Pub and Eatery in Lake Tomahawk. Barb openly admitted that she has never encountered anything paranormal in her bar. However, Barb did say that one of their long-time employees, who tends bar there, has seen a full-body apparition of a female ghost dressed all in white.

Shamrock Pub & Eatery.

"It's something we just learned to live with, doesn't seem to bother anybody or cause any harm", Barb added.

The bartender wishes to remain anonymous.

PET CEMETARY

Ole Yeller

Willie was a very well-behaved and lovable White Labrador Retriever. His coat was almost snow-white and he was broad at the shoulders. Simply put, Willie was a beautiful animal and a credit to his breed.

Willie was a loyal and faithful companion to the Dowrick family for 12 wonderful years. Chuck and Rae Dowrick live out on Dolhun Air Field, the airport just a little north of town.

Here is their story :

Rae: "This story about Willie really started before he passed away. He had a habit of making very quiet noises. It was his way of letting us know that he needed to be let out in the middle of the night. The sounds that he would emit would be like a soft, subtle whimper, you know, like, 'A little assistance here, please? I have to go to the bathroom!

"Well, after Willie died, I swear, I still could hear his little cries for help. It's as if he needed me to know that he was still here with us.

"There are also times when I still can hear him lumbering around the house, knocking into things.

"You know, he was a fairly big dog, and he'd routinely bump into stuff wherever he went. Even his tail was powerful enough to knock things down. Most of the time, it wasn't too hard to figure out what room Willie was in when he was on the move."

Rae's eyes lit up with warm memories.

I thanked Rae for her story and was about to leave.

That's when her husband, "Airport Charlie," intervened and said, "Did you tell him about the radio?"

"What about the radio?" I chimed in.

"Well, it's the strangest thing," Rae said. "Our living room radio turns on in the middle of the night, all by itself. The speakers are just blaring. Somehow the volume control gets turned all the way up. It's a bit unsettling."

"I'd say! To say the least," I said.

"Well, to get woken like this, it's enough to get my nerves unhinged. Then it's good luck trying to get back to sleep," Rae said.

"Is there a certain time of night when this occurs?" I asked.

"No, it seems to be at all different times of the night. What's consistent though, and this may sound a little weird to you…"

"What ?"

"Well, here goes. It's always a Barbra Streisand song that's playing. Always."

"Is it always the same song?"

"I don't know for sure. I'm usually still half-asleep and half-unnerved. So I can't even tell you what song it is, but I do know for certain that it's Barbra."

"Did this all start after Willie passed away?"

Rae stopped and paused for a moment, figuring out the timeline in her head. "Why, yes! Yes, it was. It was after he passed. But I'm sure the radio has nothing to do with Willie."

Well, when it comes to the paranormal, I don't know for sure, what's possible or not possible. But, then again, who does? Especially when it comes to this sort of stuff.

Maybe, just maybe, Willie was a closet Barbra Streisand fan.

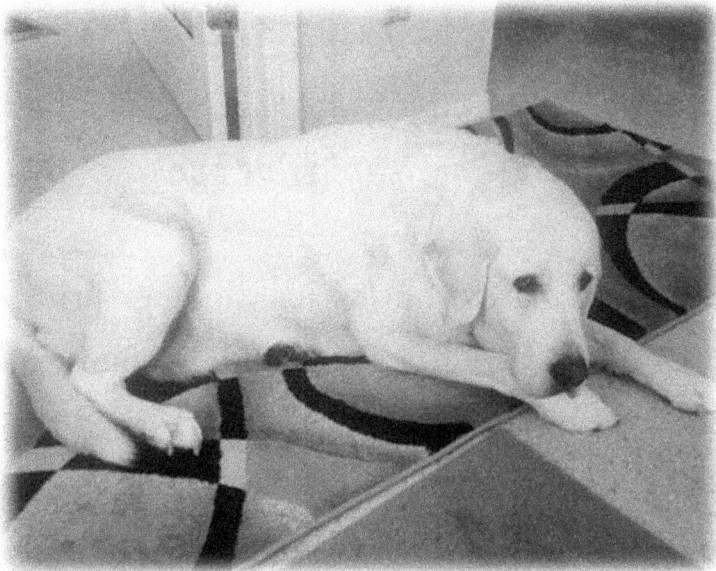

Willie daydreaming of Barbra?

Beloved Zoe

This is the initial story that sparked my interest in writing this book.

I t all started out as just another Friday night fish fry. Br. Rodd Umlauf had gotten in touch with me earlier that day to extend the invite, which by that time had become somewhat of a tradition. We'd meet on Fridays, usually at one of the local establishments. Tonight's choice was the Village Café.

This time, however, would turn out to be a little bit different.

Rodd had asked if it would be okay if a friend of his, Douglas Crow, came along for a meal and conversation.

"Sure, of course. The more, the merrier. What time are you thinking?" I responded.

"How does seven o'clock sound?"

"Seven sounds good."

"See you there."

It was a beautiful fall day in the Northwoods, but towards evening, it became somewhat stormy as a cold front pushed down from Canada. It began to downpour, which prompted us to change our plans from a "meet you there" scenario to "let's carpool together."

When the time neared, I drove over to Rodd's. His driveway was puddle-ridden from the driving rain. I had to be careful where I stepped, to dodge all the potholes and not to get a sock-full. I jumped into the back of his waiting car. Rodd put his car into gear and it was off to Doug's house.

Through the high-speed rhythm of the windshield wipers, I could barely make out the form of a person trying to keep dry beneath the overhang of the front porch.

"There's Doug. He's waiting for us." Rodd waved.

Doug jumped in the front seat and it was off to the Village Café.

We made quick introductions on the way over.

By the time we sat down for dinner, I could tell that something was troubling Doug. "You seem kind of down."

"I think I'm going crazy, " he said.

That was a pretty bold statement. *Why would he think such a thing?* I thought.

"I just lost my dog Zoe, and I'm heart-broken. I loved that dog deeply."

"What breed of dog was Zoe?"

"A King Charles Spaniel." Doug then showed me a picture of his beloved Zoe, which he wore on a chain around his neck.

I extended my condolences and added that would drive just about anybody crazy.

"That's not what's driving me crazy. I think I'm losing my mind!"

"What makes you think that," I asked.

"I swear that sometimes at night I can still feel Zoe jumping on my bed and circling down to rest."

Wow, I thought. *Now we had an instant connection.*

Douglas Crow

"You're not crazy, Doug. You're not crazy at all. I've experienced the same phenomenon many times."

Doug suddenly looked up. Our eyes locked.

"Mostly with our family dog Riley after he passed," I continued, "but even a time or two with our old farm cat, Whiskers. You know, come to think of it, when my son-in-law and our daughter's pet boxer, Lulu, passed away, even she decided to join us one night."

I went on.

"Now Lulu was no small girl. She weighed in at around 80 pounds. So when she paid us a visit, there really was no mistaking it. When she jumped on the bed, the bed shook under her weight, and as she walked over my legs, there was a downward pull of the blanket for each step she took until she'd finally circle down for one last time. So no, Doug, you're not going crazy. No, not at all. You're just very well *connected*. In all honesty, you're more *connected* than most," I said, thinking about *sensitives*.

Doug smiled.

Something down deep inside my gut told me that there was more to Douglas Crow than met the eye.

Spilled Gravy
Medical Detection Dogs

Have you ever wondered about pets having senses above and beyond those of their masters? This is one such story. Perhaps you have heard of such things, or know somebody to whom this has happened.

Our story unfolds at the old Crow's Nest, a gathering place where some of the town's elders go to meet, soak up "information," and drink their morning coffee. (AKA the BP gas station, where the old guys go every morning to bullshit and solve world problems.)

Jim Haigh had just returned from his winter hiatus in Gulf Shores, Alabama. It was the first time I'd seen Jim in about five months.

"I have a good story to tell you guys," Jim said excitedly.

My ears perked up, and we all gathered a little closer to give a good listen.

"Hans and Linda Delius came down to Gulf Shores to visit me this past winter.

"Sarah (*Jim's two-and-a-half-year-old Airedale*) kept coming up to Hans, who was wearing shorts, and sniffing Hans's leg. Hans would shoo her away, only to have Sarah return a short time later to continue sniffing in the same spot. This scenario was repeated time and time again. It got to the point where I asked Hans if he had spilled some gravy or something on his leg, to which Hans, via hand-gesture, reassured me that he hadn't."

We all chuckled at this.

"Well, anyways, a few weeks later I get a call from Hans, who now was back in Lake Tomahawk. 'You aren't going to believe this,' Hans said. 'A lump developed in the same spot where your dog was sniffing my leg, so I went to see the doctor. Turns out I have cancer in that exact spot!'"

In medical terms, Hans was diagnosed with squamous cell carcinoma and is expected a full recovery.

Now I'm not sure if this story is truly of a paranormal nature or not, but definitely a head-scratcher. A quick search and I discovered that canines have been used to detect melanoma cancer since 1989; their skills often outshine modern-day, machine-based odor analysis equipment. There has also been a high rate of success (in some studies as high as 98% to 99% accuracy) in detecting prostate cancer from urine samples.

URBAN LEGENDS

The Upper Peninsula's Ghost Train

I first found out about 93-year-old Carol Elwin from Br. Rodd Umlauf, who happens to be one of Carol's home-care providers. Rodd introduced us.

You could tell from the onset that Carol must've been some kind of live-wire back in her younger days.

There was a twinkle in her eyes as she reminisced about her past when she and her good friend, Ann Kloes, would take the drive up to Michigan's Upper Peninsula, or U.P., to check out the ghost train. She described how they would wait until just about nightfall, and then drive up Highway 45 through Eagle River going north into the

U.P., eventually making a turn-off onto Robin's Pond Road. She went on to tell how they came upon a dead-end road, next to a clearing in the woods, where the old railroad once ran. By this time in our conversation, I knew she was talking about the famous Paulding Mystery Light, on the outskirts of Watersmeet, Michigan.

After parking their vehicle, Ann and Carol would sit there in dead silence, waiting, listening, and then, there it was: in the distance, a faint unmistakable sound of the rumbling of a train approaching. The sound grew louder as the train drew near on tracks that were no longer there, reaching a deafening tone. Their car shook and rocked from side to side. Carol said she clung to the door handle for dear life as the train passed them by.

"It scared the hell out of me!" Carol said with a sheepish grin on her face.

"Oh, I almost forgot to tell you about the train's lights."

Carol went on to describe how they changed colors. First, the two friends saw a bright white light, the train's headlight, which grew brighter and larger as the train approached. Then there was a swinging red light, as if the train's brakeman was waving it from side to side, to signal the train's engineer. Sometimes when it would swing, the lantern would change colors from red to yellow then back to red again.

I asked her how long ago this all took place.

Carol replied, "Well it's been a good 40 years—seems like a lifetime ago."

I then thanked her for her time and story.

Spoiler Alert

This mystery may or may not have been debunked. Could the Paulding Mystery Light just be traffic lights? Sure, that would be a logical and plausible explanation.

I have been up there a handful of times, and have seen the light firsthand.

Though I have never heard or felt the train, Paulding never disappoints. From seeing the light to talking to curious

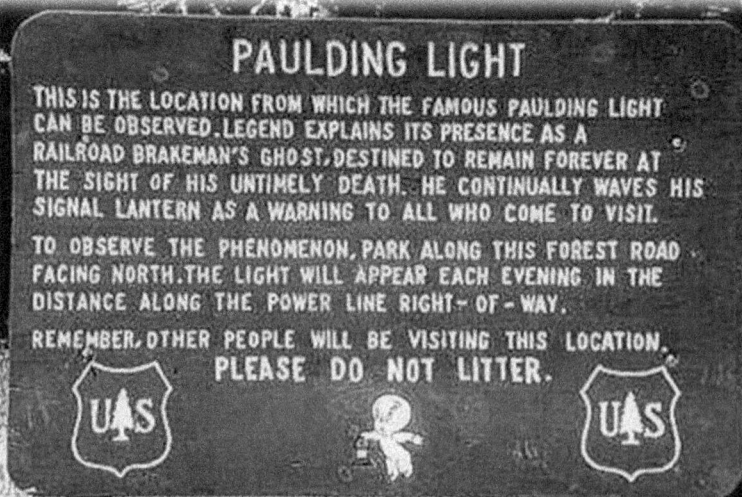

PAULDING LIGHT

THIS IS THE LOCATION FROM WHICH THE FAMOUS PAULDING LIGHT CAN BE OBSERVED. LEGEND EXPLAINS ITS PRESENCE AS A RAILROAD BRAKEMAN'S GHOST, DESTINED TO REMAIN FOREVER AT THE SIGHT OF HIS UNTIMELY DEATH. HE CONTINUALLY WAVES HIS SIGNAL LANTERN AS A WARNING TO ALL WHO COME TO VISIT.

TO OBSERVE THE PHENOMENON, PARK ALONG THIS FOREST ROAD FACING NORTH. THE LIGHT WILL APPEAR EACH EVENING IN THE DISTANCE ALONG THE POWER LINE RIGHT- OF - WAY.

REMEMBER, OTHER PEOPLE WILL BE VISITING THIS LOCATION. PLEASE DO NOT LITTER.

onlookers, there is always a certain amount of excitement in the air.

The more you talk to different people about this place, the more you get some pretty strange and unusual stories that don't fit into the "just traffic lights" scenario.

I recall one such story, in which a coworker of mine, John Peters, told me about a time when he and his girlfriend were up there in the early 1990s.

John said, "There was a sphere of light about the size of a basketball that chased us."

I asked, "What happened?"

"Well, we were sitting in our car by the dead end when this ball of light started traveling down the power lines. The ball jumped off the line and headed straight for us. I got scared and took off. That light chased my car down the road! After that, we never went back."

Then you come across a story like Carol's, and just think "Wow!" and try to connect the dots.

The Paulding Light has been featured on TV shows, including *Unsolved Mysteries*. To this very day, you still can go there, have some fun, enjoy Michigan's U.P. mystery train, and decide for yourself.

TZ's Summerwind Experience

Life's a Party

Back in our teen years, life just seemed to be one big party for many of us. It certainly rings true for Terry Zeinert of Lake Tomahawk (or "TZ" as he's locally known). His story takes place in the mid-1970s during his high school years. That's when he and his companions traveled up to the old Summerwind Mansion, located in the northern part of Vilas County, on the Wisconsin/Michigan border.

Summerwind became somewhat of a popular teen destination during the 1970s. It is often celebrated as the most haunted

site in the entire state of Wisconsin. Many articles and books have been written on this haunted place alone.

Author's recommendation: Read *The Carver Effect* by Wolffgang Von Bober, which describes experiences at Summer-wind.

The Interview

All of Terry's responses were in rapid-fire succession and matter-of-fact speaking. He remembered the times spent at Summer-wind as if they were yesterday.

TZ: Yeah, we used to drive up there [to Summerwind] back in our high school days with my sister, my cousin, and some friends. We liked to go up there and drink beer. Back then, the entire house was still standing and fully intact. There were even times when we were lucky enough to have the whole place all to ourselves."

MP (the author): "So, Terry, did you ever experience anything strange or unusual while you guys were up at the Summerwind Mansion?"

TZ: "Oh, yeah!"

MP: "Care to share some with our readers?"

TZ: "Sure! The windows in that old place would open and close all by themselves! It would be like, we just were in this room and we all could have sworn that the window was closed. Now it's opened."

MP: "Is there anything else?"

TZ: "There was also an old pool table in there. Most people don't know that."

MP: "Okay. Are there any other things you might consider to be paranormal that happened?"

TZ: "The lights. The lights would go on and off all by themselves. The funny thing is that there was no electrical power to the house"

Let that sink in for just a moment....

MP: "Please continue."

TZ: "But the strangest thing that happened to us up there, was..." Terry paused, looking me dead straight in the eyes, "was the time we took a picture of one of the fireplaces. When we finally got around to getting the film developed, we were all surprised and somewhat stunned to see the outline of what appeared to be a man standing in the fireplace; he hadn't been there when the photo was taken. I'll swear to this very day that that fireplace was empty!"

Note: At the time of this story, cameras had film that needed to be developed, a process that took a few days, unless you had your own darkroom equipment.

MP: "Do you still have that photo?"

TZ: "I think my sister does."

I thanked TZ for his time and his stories.

I did manage to track down Terry's sister. She didn't have the picture and thought that maybe her cousin did, but she did remember the photo and confirmed her brother's story.

As of this writing, I have not yet been able to get my hands on the actual photo taken by the Zeinert party.

TZ did, however, confirm that this was the same fireplace where the apparition appeared in the photo.

The Summerwind fireplace (Internet photo)

Bigfoot Bagwadjininni

Bigfoot Sighting

It was an early Sunday morning in late June of 2021. I was sleepy-headed and had shut off my alarm for the third time. *Crap*, I thought to myself, *I'm going to be late*. So I threw on a pair of shorts and some flip-flops, and off to the Lake Tomahawk Meat Market I went.

By now, you know from earlier stories that I was there first thing on Sunday mornings for their turnovers. I opened the front door to the Meat Market and immediately scanned to the right.

Good. There's still a few left. (They're best when they're still warm.)

As I waited my turn in line, I noticed a big fellow behind the counter, dressed in a customary white smock (common attire for meat market employees). For some reason, he seemed to be eyeballing me.

That's when I first met Ashley Burnett. "Who's next?" he asked.

I looked left, then right. "Must be me," I said. "A couple of turnovers, please. What flavors do you have?"

"We have apple and cherry this morning."

"One of each please."

He was now staring directly at the wrinkled t-shirt I had on from the night before.

"Skunk Ape?" he questioned.

"Yep."

We struck up a conversation about the image that was on the t-shirt.

"Yeah, it's from deep down in Florida, in the Everglades," I offered.

"I know his cousin."

Bigfoot, I assumed.

"I actually saw one up here," Ashley said.

"Really?" Now, he had my full attention.

"Yes, sir."

So naturally, I asked if he would be interested in doing an interview for my book project.

"Yes, yes I would."

"When's a good time for you?" I asked.

"I get off at 5:00."

"Sounds good. See you then."

The Interview

"Please state your name."

"Ashley Burnett."

"Are you Native American?"

Ashley: "Yes, born and raised."

"How long ago did you see a bigfoot?"

Ashley: "The summer of 2007 in the Powell Marsh in Lac du Flambeau."

"What month was it?"

Ashley: "Early June."

"What time of day?"

Ashley: "Between 3:30 and 3:45 PM."

"So plenty of daylight. Any chance of shadows playing tricks on you?"

Ashley: "No, no shadows."

"OK. Please go ahead and tell me your story."

Ashley's Story:

"I was working for the Forestry Department alongside the State Department of Fire Management preparing for a controlled burn on the Powell Marsh. I was out there building a turnaround for the fire trucks. I would lay railroad ties out into the marsh and the town would bring truckloads of dirt to me, all day long. I was scheduled until 4:30 but got done a little early around 3:30 or 3:45 and had about 45 minutes to mess around.

"So I took my tractor, a Posi-Track Cat, riding around on the marsh. I was building on the railroad grade and went out onto the dike. The dike is about four to four-and-a-half feet higher than the surrounding marsh. As I turned onto the dike facing north, that's when I saw it. I'd say it was a distance of anywhere from between 800 to 1,000 feet away."

"It walked out of the swamp and crossed over the dike. It only took two steps to cross over the dike. I was born and raised up here and I know what a bear looks like. This was no bear."

"You said it was on two legs ?" I asked.

"Yes.

"That would make it a biped," I added. "Please continue."

"I know that a bear will not cross upright on two legs over the dike. They will always cross on all four legs due to the incline. This one crossed over the dike in just two strides. That's a good eight feet," he offered.

"Even though I was well protected inside the Cat, I closed the front wind-shield. I must admit I felt a bit scared. I headed back down the dike to the railroad grade, which was around 1,500 feet away, hoping maybe to catch another glimpse of him crossing it. I waited a good five minutes and nothing. That's when my mind started to get to me. I wondered, 'Could he be in the woods watching me?'"

At 6-foot-2 and 275 pounds, Ashley Burnett is a large man, an imposing figure, not too easily intimidated.

"It simply disappeared? Interesting. I've heard that they are interdimensional beings."

"I have my thoughts on that. I think they are too," Ashley agreed.

"Have there been any other sightings out there?"

Ashley said, "Yes. I live out on White Sand Lake. My father and cousin were out fishing and they thought for sure they'd seen one that waded out in the water and was bathing. My father has since passed but my cousin is still alive. From the end of the peninsula, they could tell by the height of the trees that it wasn't a small one."

"How tall do you think the one on the dike was," I inquired.

"Around seven to seven-and-a-half feet tall. It had reddish-brown hair; it wasn't dark or black like a bear."

"Are there a lot of cedar in the swamp?" was my next question.

"Yes there are."

"That makes sense. The hair would match its surroundings. Well, this was a fascinating interview. Thank you for sharing, Ashley."

#

I had these additional questions for Ashley after the initial interview. His answers follow.

1) How long have you been working at the Meat Market?

"I've worked at the meat market for three years."

2)What do you call the Big Foot in your native language?

"We, the Ojibwe people, call them Bagwadjininni. Not pronounced the way it is spelled. We have a double-vowel language."

3.)What do you believe that they are?

"We believe that they are from here on earth, but also from space, if that makes sense. They have been here all along, by our side—humans. But we fought them, to rid them from this land. We've become scared of them for some reason or another. Some tribes believed that they took human children.

"The belief is that the star people saved them from extinction. They are highly

intelligent, more so than their human counterparts. For that said reason the aliens agreed with that assessment and decided to help. They're also capable of teleportation to and from spaceships.

"North America is key to their survival. It's the perfect breeding ground and essential to the development of their young."

Ashley Burnett talks with field investigator Pat Barney about his Bigfoot sighting out on the Powell Marsh.

REFLECTIONS
IN TIME

While this next story did not happen here in Lake Tomahawk *per se*, there is an LT connection. The couple in this story frequent our area and the author's cabin.

Every August, the annual National Antique Outboard Motor Show is hosted at Sara Park on the banks of the Wisconsin River in the Town of Tomahawk. Antique outboard enthusiasts from across the country attend the show to buy, sell, trade, and compete, as they put on display their restored antiques as fine works of art.

It's a short trip south of Lake Tomahawk on Hwy 51, about a 40-minute drive.

I go to this show just about every year to admire some of the old boats and outboard motors restorations that are on display, but mostly to go visit with old friends.

That's where I uncovered this next ghost story. What makes this story unique is the rare photographic evidence. For that reason, I decided to include it in this book.

#

While vacationing in the Black Hills of South Dakota in October of 1999, Dick and Diane Hartwig came upon a burro blocking the roadway inside Custer State Park. Here is their story. Hope you enjoy.

Dick's Story

"We were driving pretty slow, enjoying the scenery and looking at the wildlife, when we came upon this donkey standing right in the middle of the road. It was blocking our way, so of course, we stopped."

"The donkey then slowly approached our car, apparently looking for a handout, to which we kindheartedly obliged. Diane dug around the back seat and found an apple. This presented a Kodak moment so I took this picture just before rolling down the window."

"What we didn't see, however, is what was reflected in the passenger-side rear-view mirror."

"It has been said that a picture is worth a thousand words—to this we agree. It appeared to us, that in the mirror, we had inadvertently captured an image of what looks like a donkey herder from the 1800s, along with a couple of his burros. I was puzzled by this, so I had the photo blown up to make it easier to identify what was in the mirror."

He continued, "Let's put it this way, if they were really there, we would have seen them. There is no way we would have missed them. There was no one else around, nobody, not a single soul. They simply were not there!"

#

I leave this tale up to you, the reader, to decide for yourself. What do you see in the mirror?

Could this have been a residual haunting of a sort, of an old donkey herder from a different time, perhaps looking for his lost burro? Or perhaps a slip in the space-time continuum?

For a better picture of the rear-view mirror image, check out our YouTube channel at https://www.youtube.com/ @hauntedlaketomahawk.

STRANGE
ODDITIES

The Irma Vortex

The tiny town of Irma is located in the northern part of Wisconsin along the Hwy. 51/39 corridor, about eight miles north of the town of Tomahawk.

Just off of Irma's exit, there is a small display of metal art work, which included a UFO that you could see from the highway. I must have driven past that flying saucer for a good ten years. I'm sure I'm not the only one who remembers it. I used it as a man-made landmark that told me that I only had a 35-minute drive to Lake Tomahawk.

Then, on one of my weekend trips up to Lake Tomahawk, it was gone.

Did I inadvertently pass it? I wondered. Maybe I was daydreaming and drove right on past? I usually kept an eye

Author posing with the Irma UFO.

out for it, and I knew I was already north of where it should have been. *No time to investigate now*, I thought, *but on my return trip, I'll be sure to make some.*

Heading back south after a long weekend in the Northwoods always seems to sadden me, but not so much this time around. I was a man on a mission, determined to find out what happened to the saucer.

I slowed down as I approached the exit for Irma—no sign of the saucer. I signaled and turned off the freeway, then took another quick right onto the frontage road in the direction where the UFO last was.

I took the last turn, down a private drive with two huge menacing metal monster sculptures greeting me from opposite sides of the entrance. *No Trespassing* signs dotted the landscape. I hesitated for a moment, rethinking what I was getting myself into. I proceeded with caution.

This is where it got weird, like going through a time warp.

The owner had made the compound look like an old Western town. There was a boardwalk, and every building had a squared-off façade like in the 1800s. The kicker was that everything was painted flat black; it seemed like everything was in the shadows.

It was a such strange layout, straight out of the *Twilight Zone*. I again had second thoughts about this stop, but again, my curiosity got the better of me. I put the truck into park and got out.

As soon as my feet hit the ground, I heard an intimidating command. "You're trespassing! What are you doing on my property," the voice barked.

I looked, but didn't see anybody.

"I'm looking for that flying saucer that used to be here," I shouted back.

A figure emerged from the shadows.

"I sold it," he said, "Why?"

"I was just wondering what happened to it. I've driven past it for years. I really liked it—thought it was cool!"

"Are you interested?" he asked.

"I thought you said you sold it."

"I did, but the guy returned it. It's out back, behind the buildings, if you want to take a look at it."

Halloween in front of the art studio.

"Sure. Why not?" I followed, and as we went around a building, I saw the UFO sitting there in all its glory.

The guy's name was Charlie. He was the creator of the UFO.

We agreed on a price, arranged for payments, and set the date for the final pick-up.

He told me he enjoyed welding and was gracious enough to show me his workshop.

"I like your car," I said, noticing a bright yellow vehicle from the 1940s.

Charlie had sawed it in half diagonally to give it the perspective it was coming out of the corner of the building. It was a neat illusion.

Charlie turned out to be a Vietnam veteran whose main means of transportation was a old Japanese motorcycle.

"I traveled all over the country on it. I like to sleep under bridges; it cut down on my expenses," he smiled.

"That's cool," I said.

He gave me a nod.

"I'll see you in a few weeks with the rest of your money," I said and promptly left.

What a strange place, I couldn't help but think.

A couple of weeks later, I pulled into Charlie's with my last payment. It was nighttime by the time I got there. I shut off the headlights and hopped out of the truck. I couldn't believe how dark it was. It was beyond pitch black. My eyes were having a hard time adjusting.

I heard Charlie's voice coming from the boardwalk of his front porch.

My eyes caught the cherry glow from his cigarette.

"Wanna beer?" he started.

"Sure. Beer sounds good. Is it always so dark around here?" I looked skyward, noticing there was no moonlight or even a visible star in the sky.

Charlie chuckled, "That's because you're in a vortex."

"A vortex?"

"Yeah, a vortex. You've entered a dead zone. Listen." His voice trailed off.

"Listen to what? I don't hear anything," I told him.

"Exactly," Charlie said, with a measured amount of seriousness in his voice.

Not that this place isn't weird enough, I thought. *Now Charlie claims to be living in a vortex.*

About a week later, I returned to pick up the saucer with help from a neighbor, John Boeckler, never to see Charlie again.

#

The *Free Dictionary* defines a vortex as follows:

1. A whirling mass of water or air that sucks
2. A place or situation regarded as drawing into its center all that surrounds it, and hence being inescapable or destructive: *a vortex of political infighting; a vortex of despair.*

Some people believe that *vortexes* (vorticies) are how space travelers actually travel through space.

New Agers pilgrimage to Sedona, Arizona every year to visit its many vortexes.

Harvest Fest Witch

Where There's a Spark, There Isn't Always a Flame

I met Laurie Jean at the annual "Autumn on Main Street" festival, which is held every September in the Lake Tomahawk downtown district. This fest is coordinated with Tomahawk's Harley Davidson Fall Motorcycle Run. Tomahawk and Lake Tomahawk are two different places. They often get mixed up in conversation.

As you can imagine, there are tons of motorcycles in town during that time, parked up and down main street.

Next to the 4th of July, this is my favorite time of year up here.

There is something for everyone at this gathering: freshly harvested produce, homemade baked goods, brat fries, rummage sales, a car show, and more. It's really too much to list here.

It's our town's last hoorah, celebrating the end of summer before Old Man Winter descends upon the Northwoods. Excitement fills the air when the downtown becomes a hub of activity as hordes of tourists make their arrival.

While navigating through the crowd, my nose caught the delightful scent of freshly baked apple pies. The heavenly aroma drifted up into the crisp autumn air. That's when I came to an abrupt stop to avoid a big, old English Bulldog, who decided to plop down right in front of me. He stopped me dead in my tracks.

"Why, hello, big fellow." I bent over and rubbed the top of his head, looking around for the dog's owner.

Laurie Jean posing in front of the art studio.

That's when I met a brightly clad Tarot Card reader by the name of Laurie Jean. I soon found out that her personality was as colorful as her attire.

Laurie Jean had just finished setting up her display booth and apologized for her dog's behavior.

"Nothing to apologize for. He does make a pretty good speed bump, though."

We both laughed.

I instantly picked up some good vibes from her, and decided to bounce my book project off Laurie Jean to see where it would go.

"Well," Laurie Jean replied. "I don't really have any good ghost stories to share with you and your readers, but I am a practicing witch."

"Really? You're a witch?"

"A *Divination*," she added.

"If you'd like, I can share with you the time I tried to put a love spell on a male suitor of mine."

That sounded interesting. (At that moment, I was bitten by an earworm song of the 1960s, "Love Potion #9." It kept playing over and over in my head.)

"It was a concoction I made. It was supposed to help him fall in love with me. I sprinkled some onto his food. I did break down, however, and warn him ahead of time about what I had done."

She continued, "This warning didn't seem to bother him though; he must have been really hungry because he went ahead and ate it anyways. He ate the whole thing."

"So, did it work? What happened?" I asked.

"Nothing! My love potion didn't seem to have any effect on him whatsoever." she said.

"So after my love potion failed, I decided it was time to change tactics. This time around, I tried sending 'a love spark' his way, but, you know something? It was just my luck that the spark managed to boomerang itself around, right back to me. It started a ring of fire right at my feet, and I darn near got burned."

I chuckled and thanked Laurie Jean for her story.

A childhood memory jumped into my head. Laurie Jean reminded me of the zany character, Aunt Clara, who was on the 1960s hit T.V. sitcom *Bewitched.* Endearing Aunt Clara, whose spells didn't always go as planned.

Of course, the question I failed to ask Laurie Jean was: *What the heck is a "love spark" anyway?*

"Hope Keeps on Ticking"
Original artwork by Br. Rodd Umlauf

When Time Stops

Tony Goebel owned a family cottage on Dorothy Lake. He was a skilled cabinetmaker by trade. According to his daughter Linda, her father had a good friend who was a clockmaker. Together, they created a little side business of making grandfather clocks. These beautiful clocks were highly sought after, with a reputation for performing flawlessly, known for their time-keeping accuracy, and distinct chiming on every quarter hour. They were working pieces of art.

Linda stated that it was at her first communion party when it happened. The house was full of people who came to celebrate.

"One of our guests noticed that the grandfather clock in our dining room had stopped keeping time," she explained. She went on to say it had never stopped working before. "It wasn't until a few days later that we learned that the clock had stopped at the exact time and day that my dad's clockmaking friend had passed away."

The Goebel's grandfather clock.

"After that, the clock ran perfectly for another eight years, and stopped once again on the exact day and time that my father died."

To this day, the family still owns that clock, and those were the only two times that it ever stopped running—when its creators had passed away.

This story struck close to home.

I can personally relate because I had a similar experience when my own father passed away. We had a old key-wound mantel clock over our fireplace that did the

The author's mantle clock.

same exact thing. It stopped working on the same day and time that my father had passed away. To this day, I have no explanation and wonder if anybody else has had similar experiences?

Question to readers: *What do you think causes this to happen?*

Moose's Demise
Can We Foretell the future?

First I heard it—the distinct sound made me look skyward. Then I spotted it as it flew over the cabin. It was a helicopter. Not just any whirlybird but a Flight for Life 'copter. I didn't recognize its markings, but it certainly didn't look like the Spirit One Team used in this area.

I didn't find out until the next morning's coffee at the Crow's Nest that the chopper I saw was carrying a dear old friend, Carl "Moose" Willet, in a life-or-death emergency.

Quick thinking by Moose's daughter, Mary Beth Schmitz, most likely saved his life. Mary Beth is a flight RN on the crew of the Eagle 3, a response team out of Green Bay.

She was in constant ground communication with her team and summoned them to get there ASAP. (For the record, Mary has logged over 2000 flights.) She was visiting her parent's home when her dad's accident occurred, and was first to assess his injuries and administer first aid.

Moose suffered 11 broken ribs and a broken left arm when the John Deere Gator he was driving crashed into the side of a fishing pier.

Moose on the job at the Soo Line.

"Moose" was the beloved leader of Lake Hodstradt's famed Beer-Belly Boys, and for the past twenty years, had predicted his own demise. Moose proclaimed countless times through the years that he was going to be dead by the time he was 85, be it while chewing the fat during morning coffee, or knocking back a few while playing cards.

Moose was a master cribbage player, which I think was due to time spent with the Soo Line railroad, where he was employed for 40 years. I suspect that Moose had honed his cribbage-playing skills in the back of many a train's caboose.

Thanks to Mary Beth's quick actions, Moose's premonition didn't exactly come true. Moose later passed peacefully, surrounded by his family, of COVID19 at the age of 86.

Questions to the readers: *Are premonitions real? What did Moose know that we didn't? Can we actually foretell the future?*

(Actually, I'm not sure that Moose himself could answer these questions.)

MEET THE GHOSTS

Buckskin Kenny

Where do I start trying to describe Buckskin? There is just too much, so a few encounters will have to do.

I first met Buckskin while drinking coffee at the BP gas station. An old City of Milwaukee dump truck pulled in at one of the pumps to fuel up. One of the old guys I was sitting with chirped something or another about its occupant being a crazy old hermit who goes by the name of "Buckskin." This hermit had no running water or electricity on his property, and had recently had a fire at his house. I noticed the freshly cut timber in the back of his truck, which caught my interest.

"I'm going to go talk to him."

"Good luck. You're going to need it talking to that guy," was the response I got from the chorus of old-timers as they all laughed and went about drinking their coffees.

As I approached Buckskin's truck to introduce myself, I couldn't help but notice that he couldn't stay still. He was either on one side or the other of his truck, checking his tires or making adjustments to his load to ensure it wouldn't fall off. I tried to introduce myself.

"Hi, I'm Mark Palbicki." There was no response. He kept doing what he was doing, as if he hadn't heard.

I raised my voice. "Nice logs. Where'd you get them at? I'm looking for some."

"I need them," he replied. "I had a fire and need to rebuild my roof."

"Where did you buy them?"

Buckskin chuckled at that question and said, "I cut them down and peeled them myself." At that, he jumped back into his truck and was gone.

The second meeting was shortly after I purchased Old Army Pete's Lily Street cabin. The previous owner had used it for storage and there was a ton of crap to be gone through, sorted out, or hauled off to the dump. With the help of Rodd Umlauf, I managed to get the washing machine out of the cabin. We were about to load it onto a trailer, when seemingly out of nowhere came that old city dump truck. It pulled over onto the side of the road and out jumped Buckskin.

"What you going to do with that wash machine?" he asked.

"Taking it to the county dump down in Rhinelander," I replied. "Why? You want it?"

"Can I have the pump out of it?"

"Take whatever you'd like."

Figuring it was going to take him a while, I gave him fair warning. "But just to let you know, I'm going to be taking it to the dump this afternoon."

So lickety-split, he had that washing machine apart and pump out. I was impressed at how fast and seemingly knowledgeable he was. He made the disassembly look easy.

Curiosity was getting the better of me, so I asked, "What are you going to do with it?"

"I'm going to use it to pump water out of the river for my garden."

I found out later that Buckskin was a master gardener who indeed did live off his land. The old guys at coffee were only partially right. He had no electricity and no water. But I had seen enough to know he was anything but crazy. I recognize an innovative mind when I come across one.

The first time I went out to visit Buckskin on his property, it was like being in some kind of scary movie. I couldn't help but think—*all that's missing is a banjo.*

As I started down his driveway, an unsettling feeling came upon me. *What am I getting myself into this time?* As I walked further down his driveway, the smaller it became, narrowing to a single path surrounded by what I can only describe to you as junk, enough to make some salvage yards envious.

My eyes widened at the sight of a deer carcass hanging from a tree. It had been picked nearly clean to the bone. A few yards further down the path, I spied a half-skinned three- to four-pound white sucker nailed to the side of a shed. I tried to collect my nerves, while at the same time, I was half-expecting to hear that banjo strumming.

I pushed forward, calling out Buckskin's name. There was no reply. The path now branched off in several different directions, with half-buried cars, shanties, AND more dead animal remains.

Ed Gein popped into my head as my mind started to race. Maybe this hadn't been such a good idea coming back here all by myself.

I was just about ready to get the hell out of there when I saw Buckskin's head bobbing through some thickets in the distance. He was headed down the same path I was on.

Calm down. There's no music, I reassured myself.

"Buckskin," I called out. "I was beginning to think you weren't around."

"I heard your truck pull in so I went and got this for you from my garden."

In his hands was the biggest zucchini I had ever seen, and I told him so. It had to be close to four feet long.

He laughed and said, "That's nothing. I got a larger one than this still growing." So began our friendship.

Buckskin was one of a dying breed, a man who lived off the land with no running water or electricity. He was also a very well-read man who had a spectrum of different interests. The books in his library doubled as insulation in the shacks where he lived.

You could often find him along a roadside, because when his mode of transportation broke down, he simply walked from place to place, or rode a bike or his trusty garden tractor.

If I had ever been asked the question, "If you were in a plane crash and stranded in the wilderness, who would be the one person you know that you would want with you to ensure your survival?"—my answer would undoubtedly be Buckskin.

"Bucky," as I liked to call him, wasn't perfect. Many times, he was

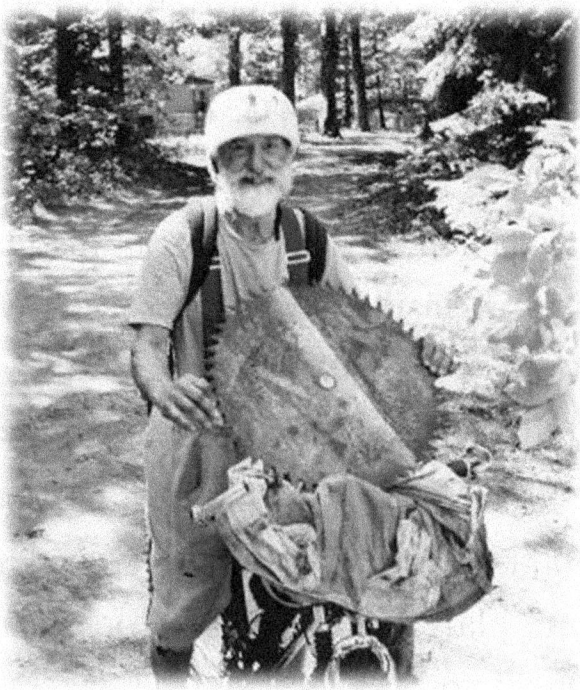

Buckskin sporting his Northwood's fashion

misunderstood, especially when it came to picking up stuff he thought he might have future use for. That sometimes got him into trouble.

I'm no doctor but he may have been suffering some sort of paranoia disorder.

"He was a man with a plan," Br. Rodd Umlauf used to say.

Buckskin had many endearing qualities about him and was definitely a part of the fabric that makes up Lake Tomahawk.

Jimmy Soyck

How would one describe Jimmy Soyck? I'd say, in a nutshell, Jimmy Soyck was Mr. Lake Tomahawk personified. If Lake Tomahawk were a person, it'd most probably have been the likes of Jimmy Soyck.

Now he wasn't perfect. He had his faults, and was even troubled at times. It was sometimes hard to figure out why he did things the way he did. That said, he was friendly, generous, outgoing, and had a way about him that was just plain likable. I'm sure all those who knew him have their own stories to tell about Jimmy.

Jimmy was one of the first people I met up here. I walked into his tavern, sat down, ordered a beer, and introduced myself. He had me sign his guest registry the day we met. Our friendship lasted to his end, and come to think of it, maybe beyond. He made me feel welcomed and accepted to our small community from the get-go. To me, this was of utmost importance in choosing an area in which to settle.

Jim was the owner and proprietor of the Happy Daze Tavern. He was an old high school jock from South Milwaukee, who

Br. Rodd Umlauf (L) and Jimmy Soyck (R) hamming it up

played hard and drank even harder. Jimmy was also the play-by-play announcer for our beloved Snowhawks Snowshoe baseball team. So to speak, he was our own Bob Uecker of the Northwoods.

Dona Kloes

I first met Dona in one of the bars in Lake Tomahawk. She was either tending bar or sitting on the bar stool across from or next to mine. Either way, I soon found out that she could hold her own in an intelligent conversation, and on just about any topic that would come up (and mind you now, without easily being offended).

She may have experienced some social injustice in our small town, where one could easily be ground up in the local grist mill of rumors, or worse yet, be pigeon-holed as something or somebody you are not.

The kindest words may not always have been spoken about her, but Dona's closest friends knew that she was smarter, stronger, and deeper than most gave her credit for. Through it all, Dona stood tall, or maybe— I should say she *leaned* a little bit—she liked to drink, and in her own right, could more than hold up her end in that category as well.

I used to bring back my cousin Alvin's homemade wine from the family farm in the deep south part of Indiana, or "Kentuckiana," as locals like to refer to it. It quickly became one of Dona's beverages of choice. She just loved it! At times, I wasn't sure if she was happier to see me or cousin Alvin's wine. We became drinking buddies.

"Nothing else that I've ever tried has had the same effect on me," Dona once told me.

The secret was that the wine was fermented in old Early Times whiskey barrels, which not only affect the wine's flavor but also its potency. Cousin Alvin fondly called it "wineshine."

"Where are you from originally, Dona?" I asked one evening.

"Milwaukee's old Polish north side."

"You're kidding! So am I. Of course, nowadays it's known as the ever-popular 'Riverwest' neighborhood."

We both chuckled. This cemented our long friendship.

If Jimmy Soyck and Buckskin were part of the town's fabric, then Dona was part of the thread that helped bind it together.

Noteworthy: Dona was also the only person I ever knew who had her funeral music preplanned way in advance. I'm kind of foggy on the timeline on when she told me about this playlist, but it was a good few years before her untimely death. Unfortunately, I can only remember a couple of the songs she picked out. One was

"Imagine" by John Lennon and another was "It's a Wonderful World" by Louie Armstrong.

Dona went on later in life to become the owner of the Village Café…which led us to my team's first paranormal investigation.

GHOST HUNTS

Kicks and Giggles

What I'm about to share inadvertently became my first investigation.

I had recently purchased a ghost app online, *ProVox Ghost Box*. I had heard about it on the "Coast to Coast" radio program, hosted by George Noory. The station also mentioned the *Ghost Box* on podcasts like *Real Ghost Stories OnLine* and Jim Harold's *Campfire*.

I wanted to find out for myself what all the excitement with this ghost box app was about, and bought it from the app store. I immediately tried it out at my home in Slinger, Wisconsin. Much to my dismay, nothing happened. I thought to myself, *Sucker, you've just been had ... more money just wasted.*

I had gotten into a bad habit of taking my iPad with me everywhere I went, so naturally it was with me when I went back up to Lake Tomahawk to our old cabin. I thought for kicks and giggles that I would try my new ghost app out up there.

Within the first hour, I got my very first hit on the app. The name *Edward* appeared in the box. That was followed by the name *Roy*, and finally a surname of *Christansen*.

After that, the box went silent—no more hits for the rest of the day.

I was skeptical about what had just occurred, but excited at the same time, if that makes any sense.

That same day Roy Umlauf had visited the cabin to pay me for some muskies baits I had made for him. (The ghost box was turned on.) My logical brain told me that perhaps there was some sort of spyware associated with this app and that was where the name Roy came from.

Christansen happened to be the surname of a recently deceased neighbor who shared a road easement on my property. This was puzzling to me. Could that just have been a coincidence?

And finally, the only explanation for the name Edward I could come up with, would be that of my Uncle Eddie, who used to stop up and visit before he passed away.

Later that evening, I stopped over at Br. Rodd Umlauf's house and told him what I had been up to, to which he responded that the name Edward was in fact his brother Roy's middle name.

"No way!" I fired back in disbelief.

I dug into my back pocket. Roy had paid me with a check. Sure enough, there it was—his middle name was Edward. Maybe there's something to this app, I was beginning to wonder? Or maybe it was my mind playing tricks on me. Either way, it was starting to pique my interest.

The Village Café

Dona's Dimes

Owners of the Village Café, Eric Kloes and his wife Jessica, believe that Eric's deceased mother, Dona Kloes, the prior owner of the Café, is now haunting the restaurant. According to Eric, his mother has been "leaving dimes in the strangest of places, like in a bucket of water, or on a freshly cleaned-off table." Eric has even found dimes under the oven he normally uses. Just to name a few.

Eric Kloes, Dona's son

Team's 1st Investigation

Location: Lake Tomahawk, WI
Place: Village Café
Date: Sept. 28th, 2018
Investigators:
    Jeff Braun
    Pat Barney
    Mark Palbicki
Time: 9:00 PM/10:30 PM

Evidence:

1) 2 hits on temperature range instrument
2) 3 words on ProVox Ghostbox:
    Maybe
    Village
    Girl
3) One knock on wall while playing the Bread CD

Possible Explanations:

1) Temperature instrument was moved from dining area into back kitchen area and needed time to acclimate. Kitchen was cooler than dining area, checked by Jeff Braun.

2) ProVox app. is used for entertainment purposes only, no scientific backing, and not hooked up to a radio to scan the white noise. Pat Barney reports.

3) Knock is plausible. Was it possibly the coffee maker heating water? All three investigators responded to it. It was a fairly loud knock on the south wall behind the counter. Source of the sound was never discovered.

   EVPs (Electronic Voice Phenomenon) were attempted, but none were recorded— too much background noise. Need to retry at a later date. Mark Palbicki reports.

Conclusion: There are more questions than answers.

#

There had been a string of what one would call bad-luck occurrences befalling the Café in recent months. Our findings could have easily pointed to the them being only coincidental, but were they? The night the investigation took place, the Café had a massive drainage problem, causing it to close for several days for repairs. There was a different type of energy on the premises the evening of the investigation.

Different "trigger" mechanisms were used during this investigation to draw out any spirits that might have been in the area. These included: CDs of Dona's funeral songs, Buckskin's tribute, the musical group Bread, a bottle of Dona's favorite homemade wine, and a can of Dona's favorite beer.

Dona Kloes

The investigation was inconclusive, but to be continued....

Questions:

1) Where are the dimes coming from?
2) Can the string of bad luck be attributed to a haunting?
3) Is the ProVox app a hoax? (Wondering if it's an electronic *Ouija Board* or an *Ovilus* of some sort, or mic'd with spyware? It did spell out "maybe village girl" in that order. We were looking for Dona, and she did own the Village Café. This app. likes to play with your mind.)

Since this investigation, I can't tell you how many *dimes* I've found. I'm wishing Dona had collected silver dollars!

A side note: In life, Dona believed her house was haunted. I had first-hand experience there with a lamp giving me a shock that nearly knocked me off my feet. I discovered it wasn't plugged in. This wasn't a static shock, in my experience—it was a shock from a live current.

American Legion Post 318.

Spirit of American Legion Post 318

Summer 2017
Investigators:
Mike Chevalier
Mark Palbicki

M ike Chevalier approached me one day and asked if I would be interested in doing a paranormal investigation at American Legion Post 318.

"Funny you asked. I just picked this new Ghostbox app on my iPad and would love to try it out," I told him. Naturally I jumped at the opportunity. "What type of activities are going on?"

"Mostly poltergeist," he said, "with the most common being the dragging of chairs across the main hall all by themselves, but there also been the sounds of somebody walking up and down the staircase with nobody there and electrical lights shutting on and off by themselves."

Later that evening, Mike and I spent a few hours investigating Post 318.

I witnessed for myself a light going on and off at this first investigation.

From the initial investigation of Post 318, the ProVox app has gone ballistic, with the word-storage page maxing out on several different occasions. This happened on the very next day after the 318 investigation while at my cabin. I'm having a hard time giving this app any merit but at the same time, can't explain the how and why of it. This prompted me to research paranormal equipment.

August 5th, 2019

According to American Legion Post 318 Commander Gary Madden, when questioned about the paranormal activity at the 318. "Yes, there is," he agreed, and went on to say that they actually knew the name of one the ghosts.. He was a Korean War veteran by the name of Nahum who had also been an active member of Post 318 before his passing. "He liked to go down stairs and play pool," Gary added.

\#

2nd investigation
August 7th, 2019

Investigators:
    Br. Rodd Umlauf
    Patrick Barney
    Scot Mortier

Jeff Braun

Mark Palbicki

Mike Chevalier

Evidence:

1) EM meter going off for no apparent reason

2) EMF meter spiking (all within a 12-foot radius from floor to ceiling, forming a energy column) in front of glass case in the main meeting hall.

3) Several cold spots were noted in the meeting hall as well. The temperature gauge recorded a drop of 4 degrees.

4) Orbs and rods observed. All orbs and rods have been debunked as flying insects.

5) Kinect camera was trying to form an object within the 12-foot energy column.

6) A ceiling fan turned on by itself.

7) Trifield natural meter spiked a few times that night and when tested with a volt meter the next day, the battery actually had a higher

reading than before the investigation. Somehow the battery inside the Trifield meter managed to increase in strength. This was puzzling .

The 318 also holds some history back in the lumber company days when the town still had a constable. The 318 was used as a drunk tank and jail and was referred to as the "Rainbow House."

Equipment used :
- Trifield Natural EM Meter
- P-Tec EMF Meter
- Seismograph
- Nethertech Hot/Cold Deviation Detector
- ITC Dual Sweep Frequency Research Device P-SB 11
- Infrared Thermometer
- Panasonic RR-QR200 EVP Recorder

- Ghost Hunter Infrared Audio/Video Capture Device
- HT-175 Thermal Imager
- Kinect camera
- EMF Adjustable Pump

ProVox Ghostbox Hits:
1) seamless
2) deal
3) car
4) Moore
5) see
6) late
7) eleven

Summary:

I find that Lake Tomahawk's American Legion Post 318 is supercharged with emotional energy. This type of energy is often referred to as *telekinesis* or *psychokinesis*.

Could this emotional residue be the contributing factor to the poltergeist activities that have been reported by its membership ?

Could the column of energy we encountered be attributed to what are known as *Ley Lines*?* I could not find any maps that could substantiate this theory.

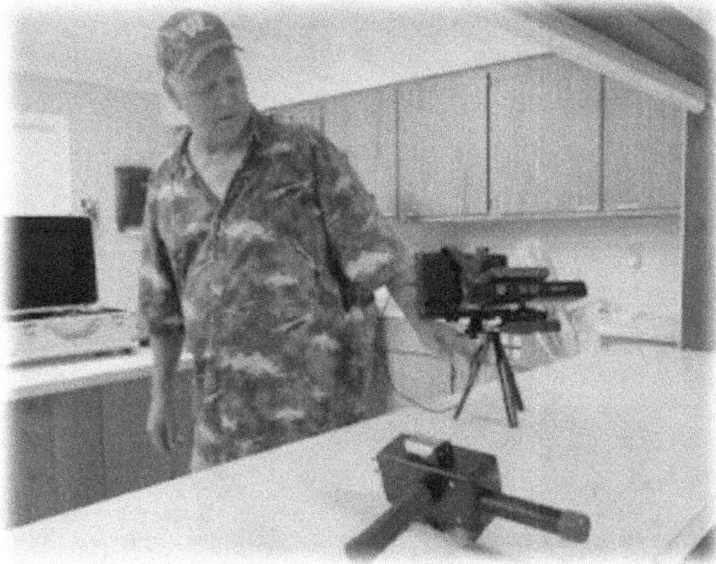

Author setting up the Kinect camera

---

* Ley lines are lines that crisscross around the globe, like latitudinal and longitudinal lines, that are dotted with monuments and natural landforms, and carry along with them rivers of supernatural energy. (Source: *Ley Lines, The Supernatural Lines That Connect The Universe* (allthatsinteresting.com)

Pat Barney and Jeff Braun waiting to enter

Br. Rodd Umlauf preparing protection for
the night's investigation

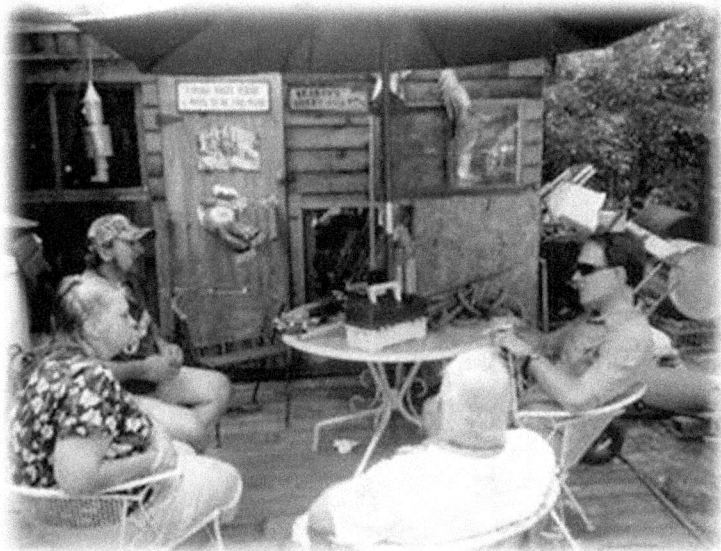

Fulcrum Team Member Scot Mortier interviews
Michael Chevalier prior to Post 318 investigation

Investigation at the Lill's

This investigation took place at Wendell and Elly Lill's residence.

Lake Tomahawk
Date : September 26th, 2019

Investigators:
    Pat Barney
    Jeffery Braun
    Mark Palbicki
    Assisted by Carl Koyn

Equipment used:
EMF meter P-TEC
Thermo imager hand held
ProVox Ghost Box
Seismograph
Trifield Natural Meter
Panasonic RR-QR200 EVP Recorder

After the interview with Rainer Lill, their son, he agreed to let us do an investigation at his residence.

I knew from the onset that this was going to be a long shot, because everything I had ever read or studied about poltergeist activity indicated the contributing catalyst or agent usually must be present at the scene in order to have any activity.

.

Investigators Jeff Braun and Pat Barney

Our investigation there proved fruitless. There were no hits or abnormalities registered on any of our paranormal equipment that day.

Carl assists Jeff during the investigation

Investigation of Buckskin's Property

Investigators:

Br. Rodd Umlauf

Mark Palbicki

Location : Lake Tomahawk

Place: Ken Garbisch river property

Date: October 31st, 2018

Time 5:15/7:30-9:20/9:30

Equipment used:

- EMF meter P-TEC
- Trifield Natural EM Meter
- Seismograph
- P-SB11 sweep spirit box
- Airline response ghost box
- Panasonic RR-QR200 EVP recorder
- Catch a ghost Yes/No Analyzer

- EMF pump
- ProVox ghostbox app.

Evidence:

1) Heavy frost on Yes/No Analyzer, air temperature was too warm to produce frost at the time of occurrence. No other frost or areas of frost were observed at location. Air temperature teetered between 39 and 40 degrees. 32 degrees is need to produce frost. Presence of my own breath could not be seen.

2) Ghost Box Portal volume was somehow manipulated?
   Possible explanation: Analyzer was accidentally left behind from initial investigation, was at location for about an additional two hours. Temperatures reached freezing point later that night.

   No evidence was observed on any other paranormal devices.

3) ProVox app. recorded no words.
   Note: Rodd Umlauf could hear Response
   Box while we were on opposite side of
   property approximately 4 to 5 acres in distance away. At the volume at which it was
   set, it would be impossible to hear it from that
   far away. I had intentionally lowered the
   volume to not draw any unwanted attention
   from the road.

Questions:
1) Can an entity change or manipulate the
   volume control on the response box?
2) Can an entity affect the temperature enough
   to cause frost on our equipment?
3) Air temperature reading was 40 degrees. No
   other items in surrounding area had any frost
   on them.

Follow-up :

Answer to 1). I emailed maker of response box about said event: "Sounds like a spirit did mess with your volume."

Answer 2): While attending a paranormal conference in southwest Florida, I questioned the appearance of frost on the analyzer, in which a panel of professional researchers said that it absolutely possible.

On site, Br. Rodd Umlauf using EMF meter at Buckskin's property

I had tried to repeat the appearance of frost by experimenting later that same night and the next two following evenings, without any success. Even though the temps where colder, I could not get that meter to frost over.

Conclusion:

Even though a piece of equipment had acquired a thick layer of frost on it, and Rodd could hear the response box from a good distance away, I concluded that there was no activity that would be deemed as paranormal going on at this location at this time. But something strange did happen after this investigation, as you will read in the "Bucky Follows Me Home" story.

#

2nd Investigation

October 31st 2019 /
10:00AM/12:00PM

Investigator:

    Mark Palbicki

Equipment used:

- EMF Meter P-TEC
- Mel Meter MEL-REM-ATDD
- Trifield Natural EM meter

Mel meter placed in the scar of a tree

I decided to go back out to Buckskin's property after learning that his son Jeff had recently spread his father's ashes there. The only clue I had to Buckskin's whereabouts was that the ashes had been spread out by a tree near the river. I was flying solo on this investigation so I packed light with only a few pieces of paranormal equipment in tow.

Having limited equipment, it proved a daunting task to decide where to place the tools. There were just too many trees by the river.

I decided to place the Mel meter in the scar of a large tree where it would be easily visible from a central location. When I put the Tri-field meter in the last location, it was maybe 10 minutes later when the Mel meter went off, lighting up like a Christmas tree.

It stayed lit for about 15 to 20 seconds, then shut off, then lit fully again for about another 5 seconds. I fumbled to start my iPad to make a video recording, but by the time I had it booted up, all of the activity was over.

This Mel meter has a REM feature on it, which creates its own EM field. It is designed to light up only when the field is entered. I remained there for a couple more hours, but that was the only activity I encountered. I took a picture of the tree and later sent it to Buckskin's son Jeff. Jeff confirmed that indeed that was the same tree where his Father's ashes had been spread.

Observations and Questions:

1) What caused the Mel meter to light up? I did not have my cell phone at this location and my IPad was shut off, so they are ruled out. I did not see any squirrels or birds or anything else that might have triggered the device. There is no electrical power at this location.

2) What were the chances of my finding the cor-
rect tree where Buckskin's ashes had been
scattered? Was it a coincidence?

X Marks the Spot
In search of Pete Ryan

I first met Pete, out of the blue, when he showed up at my cabin. He had the most electric personality I've ever encountered. He was a real-life version of the movie character, Jerry McGuire.

He introduced himself, and then complemented me on the work I was doing on the old cabin.

"What you've got here," he said, "is a labor of love."

Before I knew what hit me, this guy knew where I lived, where I worked, what I did for a living, and what my hobbies were. I can't repeat enough how much Pete was a human dynamo.

By the time our conversation was over, I found myself driving Pete to his home in

Cascade. Before that ride was to be over, however, we found ourselves surrounded by police with their firearms drawn and at the ready.

It was on Hwy 43, just south of Green Bay, where we got *escorted* by three squad cars to the shoulder of the road: one in front, one behind, and one on the driver's side.

All of them had their emergency lights on and sirens blaring. It was enough to get your heart pumping, if you know what I mean. The long and the short of it was, Pete and I fit an APB (all-points bulletin) for armed robbery suspects in the area!

After a few tense moments and showing our proper IDs, we were cleared and back on our merry way again. I apologized to Pete shortly after our unexpected stop, for a bad thought that he was the reason we were getting pulled over and I was going to have to explain to the police how I really didn't know the guy sitting next to me in the passenger seat.

Pete laughed and said, "You know, I was thinking along the same lines about you."

Now we both were laughing and so began a long friendship.

#

I didn't think this story would make it into this book. Pete Ryan was on my short list of prospective investigations, but time was running out and my deadline for publication was looming near.

As serendipity would have it, I ran into Pete's youngest son, Owen, and his mother Linda one day in front of the Lake Tom art studio.

Owen had grown into a man since I had last seen him at his father's funeral five years ago.

"It's good to see you, Owen."

"You too, Mark."

"What brings you guys out here?" I asked.

"We came to spread my father's ashes— Lake Tomahawk was his favorite place," he said.

I nodded in agreement, then pulled him aside to ask, if he didn't mind, where his father's final resting place might be.

"When we were kids, my dad drew us up a treasure map, with hints and clues on it to find a buried treasure. We made a game out of it," he explained. "So, along with my brother Antone and my sister Maria, we went out on a treasure hunt around Dorothy Lake," he continued. "I thought it would be fitting for Dad's final resting place to be where the hidden treasure was, *where X marked the spot.*"

Pete's passing had caught us all by surprise. A super-aggressive cancer had taken our good friend away, way too soon.

Br. Rodd Umlauf never got the chance to attend his funeral or to say his final goodbyes. When I told him about Owen, Rodd stopped me mid-sentence, "I remember that map. I was in on it, many years ago. I think I know where Pete's at."

"What do you say? Let's take that old wooden boat of yours out and pay him our last respects," Rodd said.

"You bet. Pete loved fishing out of that old boat. Let's give our dear ol' friend a final send off," I answered.

We launched the boat and headed off in search of Pete Ryan. When we finally reached our destination, Rodd gave a short sermon about Pete, his love of life, and his many passions. He followed it with a final blessing.

With prior success came high hopes that once again, we would find some sort of *strange frequencies* at Pete's final resting place. Unlike with Buckskin, however, we neither found nor sensed any signs that Pete was still around. But knowing Pete, he probably hit the ground running on the other side. As you can see, not all ghost hunts are successful, but it was good to say our final goodbyes.

Pete with a nice Canadian musky.

Village Café
Second Investigation
The Afterglow Party

August 18th 2022, 8:00PM.

Investigators:

    Pat Barney

    Jeff Braun

    Mark Palbicki.

    Special guest: Tom Cattani, filmmaker.

Equipment used:

    Everything in my arsenal.

It was almost hard to believe the great job Eric and Jessica did on their remodeling of the Village Café, especially the transformation in the basement, which was practically unrecognizable from our last investigation there.

We started off as we usually did by checking out what was emitting EMF fields on site, taking temperatures, checking windows, doors, vents and anywhere drafts might occur, which could affect our temperature gauges.

We discovered that a baseboard heating system surrounding the dining area was emitting EMF readings.

We began setting up our equipment in the basement and kitchen. In the basement, we noticed that the LED ceiling lights were flickering. I placed a Mel meter, with the REM feature, up on a bread shelf and within minutes, we had a mid-range hit on it.

I later tested the shelf with the EMF meter and couldn't detect any electrical fields that would cause the Mel meter to trigger. Meanwhile, I was called upstairs by investigator Jeff Braun to help interpret the image he was receiving on the handheld thermo imager.

Pre-investigation run-through:

Before all of our investigations, we do a
preliminary equipment check as follows:
1) Battery replacement (new) plus voltage check
2) Check proper working condition of equipment
3) Refresher course on equipment usage
4) Mental inventory on equipment locations.

Pictured here from L to R: Investigators
Pat Barney, Jeff Braun, and Tom Cattani

"Look at this!" On the screen appeared to be the shape of a person working behind the counter. I could indeed see something, not sure what to make of it, but just then Tom Cattani shouted for me to check out the EM Trifield Natural meter that was maxed out.

We had gathered on the dining room side of the counter. Jeff now had the Thermo Imaginer upside down on the countertop, aiming it towards the back side of the counter. Pat and I were discussing getting the Kinect camera ready when Tom excitedly announced that the EM Trifield Natural meter was wigging out again.

At that exact moment, a loud pop sounded and the bank of lights over the booths (5 to 6 lights in total) went out. We all jumped and immediately stared at each other. The looks on our faces must of been priceless, especially our team's biggest skeptic for that evening, Pat Barney, whose eyes were about to jump out of their sockets.

What the hell just happened? we were thinking.

Our first thoughts were that a breaker had blown, but the pop had been much too loud and too close to have come from the basement where the breaker box is located. We checked the breakers and all were in good working order. Next we checked out the light switches, and found the one associated with the booths. We turned it off and on a few times, but it was no longer in working condition.

I must admit at this point excitement filled the air.

Pat had the Kinect camera fired up and ready to go. Jeff quickly volunteered to operate it. I reminded him that the monitor was actually mirrored so what was on its left was actually on its right and visa versa. I instructed Jeff to make sure to eliminate any and all objects and structures that might give a false image. (This type of camera will try to make stick images out of things like stools, table and chairs, booths, etc.....)

"Double-check to be sure. Here, aim it at Tom's tripod," I said. "Yep, it's making a stick image. O.K. Be careful."

Well, it didn't take long before Jeff picked up a stickman image, then another and another.

"What do you make of this one?" he asked.

It was a *spider-looking one* that seemed to be crawling on the floor, closely following a more erect stick image. Another one appeared behind the counter, and one even followed me around as I walked down the main aisle.

"Mark, there's one right next to you on your left. No, your other left." Jeff directed.

I put my arm out to wrap around the shoulder of whoever or whatever that was.

Jeff sounded out, "It just ducked under your arm."

Whatever this was, it was now interacting with us.

"Let me take a look, Jeff," I said and we watched for a while as a stick image seemed to be doing some sort of "I'm here" performance for us.

"Dona, is that you?" Jeff questioned.

Instantaneously, the entity vanished. We both turned towards each other. *Wow, was that just a coincidence?*

Then a thought hit me like a ton of bricks. That spider-looking entity Jeff described earlier could very well be an animal. In fact, the way it followed the upright figure reminded me of a dog. OMG, could that be *Puppers*, Buckskin's loyal companion?

I started questioning myself. *Is my imagination getting the better of me?*

Tom Cattani and Jeff Braun went back down into the basement. A short time later, they called me to come downstairs. Two more stick images had appeared in the center of the refrigerator room.

I turned on the lights and on saw a French fry maker on the table to the left. "Well, here's your stickman," I teased.

Jeff turned the camera towards the French-fry maker and replied, "I don't think so."

It wasn't until our return trip home when Tom informed me that when he and Jeff were down in the basement, Jeff asked the stick image a question: "Buckskin, is that you?"

"Mark, I'm telling you that thing instantly disappeared. It was unbelievable," Tom said.

Now, Tom and I had both witnessed similar experiences with Jeff and the Kinect camera. Was this just a peculiar coincidence or was there something more in play going on here. *Could it be a confirmation? A verbally repeated question/response experiment?*

We were lucky enough to capture both incidents on camera. Decide for yourself at https://www.youtube.com/@hauntedlake-tomahawk.

Jeff Braun sure seemed to be the *go-between* on this evening. Later, Jeff admitted that he felt like he was being *pulled* into the paranormal activity. *Like I was becoming the medium.*

We were fortunate enough to have filmmaker Tom Cattani present on this investigation, so hopefully he caught enough footage to put together a short little clip of what transpired that evening. Be sure to check it out. (https://www.youtube.com/@hauntedlaketomahawk).

Now usually my investigation summaries are written to be a bit on the dry side, stating the facts, equipment used, weather conditions, times, blah, blah, blah. But seeing how this was to be my paranormal team's last investigation, I thought it only proper to keep true to the title of this book and romanticize it as a true ghost story.

HAUNTED LAKE TOMAHAWK

Summary:

The romantic in me would like to think that on August 18th, 2022 at the Village Café, we witnessed one last going-away party, an *Afterglow Party,* if you will. My paranormal team and I were the guests.

The ghost hostess with the mostess, was of course Dona Kloes, the previous Café owner. I got the feeling she was finally happy and satisfied with the progress her kids had made with the old café.

Our special guests that evening included the ghosts of Buckskin Kenny and his dog Puppers, who walked into town to pay us a parting visit before heading off into the great unknown Northwoods in the sky.

And last, but not least, behind the counter in this all-too-familiar setting (tending bar), was none other than the ghost of the one and only Jimmy Soyck, appearing happy as a clam, to be serving up his last customers. "Yeah, Baby!"

You had to be there to witness all the para-normal activities that happened. Then you would know that this story really isn't too much of a stretch of the imagination, in fact, it's just a matter of connecting the dots.

Happy Hauntings!

Booo!

PERSONAL
EXPERIENCES

"BUCKY" FOLLOWS ME HOME

The following pages portray the author's first-hand experiences with Buckskin Kenny.

From the onset, I had already decided that I was only going to do paranormal investigations of people whom I knew and were friends with in life. My reasoning was that of caution, the "just-in-case" scenario. You know, just in case, there was a remote possibility that something could go wrong and that something could become malicious or ill-attached. I figured if I was good with these folks in life, I'd be good with them in death. So goes this story.

It started after the investigation on "Buckskin" Kenny's property on

Halloween 2018 that paranormal team member Br. Rodd Umlauf and I had performed.

1st Experience

The first time something "funny" happened was shortly after I returned to my residence in Slinger. The very next day, in fact, after the Buckskin Halloween investigation.

I'd gotten an early start on the day for the trip home from Lake Tomahawk, timed to arrive around midmorning. As I age, I find that I'm not a big fan of driving in the dark anymore. I pulled into our driveway, hit the clicker to open the garage door, and proceeded into the house.

My wife, Donna, greeted me at the door, gave me a big hug, and told me how much she'd missed me. "How was your drive back?"

"Uneventful. (*which is a good thing*) It was pretty much smooth sailing…"

"You look tired."

"Yeah, was a long drive…."

"Why don't you put us on a pot of coffee?"

"You bet!" That was more than a welcome suggestion.

Innocently enough, that's when "it" started, while I was attempting to make a fresh pot of coffee. I went into the kitchen, ground some beans, filled the coffee machine with water, and proceeded to brew some coffee.

After about 15 minutes, I heard, "Hey, that coffee should be just about done by now. Could you be as so kind as to pour me a cup?" Donna shouted from her lofty perch in the upstairs study, where she was working on her computer.

"Yeah, you got it." I grabbed her favorite coffee mug from the kitchen cupboard and proceeded to the coffee maker to pour her a hot cup of joe.

That's when I noticed that there was no coffee in the coffee pot and that the brewing process hadn't even begun. *Hmm, that's funny.* I could have sworn I turned the machine on. I distinctly remember the little LED indicator light located on the power switch being lit when I had pressed it earlier. So I pressed it again. This time no light came on at all.

Just then, Donna shouted down, "Hey, how's that cup of coffee coming along?"

I shouted back up to her, "I think the coffee maker's shot. It's not working. Oh, wait, I found the problem."

"What's going on?"

"It wasn't plugged in."

"Yeah, that would help," Donna snickered.

"Smart aleck," I whispered under my breath.

Granted, I was tired from the drive, so I didn't think twice about it.

2nd Experience

The next morning, Donna was up early and decided to go downstairs and make the coffee. I could faintly make out the sound that the coffee grinder makes as she ground up some freshly roasted beans. There's a pretty simple routine we follow: grind the coffee beans, replace the filter, add the water, place coffee in filter, and turn on the machine. Usually by the time the heavenly aroma hits the upstairs bedroom, a full pot is just about done.

But not this morning. This morning, it was my turn to wait.

"Oh, very funny," Donna shouted up, "Very funny!"

"What? What's so funny?"

"When did you come downstairs and unplug the coffee maker?"

"What?"

By now, you might have figured out that I'm hard of hearing.

"When did you come down and unplug the coffee?"

"It wasn't me. I'm still up here," I called down from the bedroom.

"Sure, very funny, ha-ha."

"Hey! I haven't even gotten out of bed yet."

"Sure!"

A short time later, Donna came up the stairs with a hot cup of coffee. "Very funny," she persisted.

After I reassured Donna for the umpteenth time that I had nothing to do with unplugging the coffee pot, we tried to use logic and reason things out, instead of pointing fingers at each other.

"Well, maybe our cat Izzy unplugged it," Donna suggested.

This is where I must describe how the coffee maker is plugged in. The cord to the coffee maker is plugged into a short strip of outlets on about a six-inch pigtail. So in order to unplug it, one has to hold down the power strip and pull on the cord. I don't think Izzy is capable of unplugging it. I did some experiments on unplugging the coffee pot and determined that you need both hands and opposing thumbs to do it.

3rd Time's a Charm

This took place only a couple of days after the 2nd occurrence.

After we had had our fun, we called a truce and stopped accusing each other of unplugging the coffee maker. After all, on the 3rd day, nothing happened and morning coffee went as planned.

But on the 4th day, that damned coffee maker once again had unplugged itself after we had started the brewing process. This time, we realized that we weren't having fun at each other's expense and that perhaps something strange was going on. At that point, we were both starting to get a little weirded out by what was happening.

I had a gut feeling that perhaps my old pal "Buckskin" was playing tricks on us. I let Donna know my thoughts on this, and she said, "I just don't know…"

Later that same morning, we decided to go grocery shopping. As we were walking down an aisle, Donna suddenly froze in her tracks so fast that I failed to notice and walked a few steps ahead of her. That's when I noticed a loaf of bread lying on the store's floor a good six to seven feet away from the nearest shelf.

"Is this ours?"

"Mark! Mark!" Donna repeated with a bit of apprehension in her voice, as I walked over to pick up the loaf.

"What?"

"Didn't you see?"

"Uh, didn't I see what?"

"That loaf of bread flew off the shelf all by itself!"

"No, I didn't see, I was looking the other way, toward the beer aisle. But, by judging the distance, there was no way it just fell off the shelf by itself."

"No, it didn't fall," Donna insisted. "It flew! It flew right off the shelf like some-body threw it!" This shook Donna up quite a bit.

I went over and checked out the shelv-ing. It had a solid back. Checked to see how the loaves were stocked; they were stacked two high. I determined that the loaf of bread couldn't have fallen off the shelf the way Donna had described.

So much so, that I made the point out loud. "O.K. Bucky, I know Donna was one of your favorites but knock it off! You're scaring her!" Ironically, after that outburst, the activity stopped.

Donna actually went out and bought a new coffee maker after these events.

Buckskin at the ruins of the
famed Summerwind

And Again

About a year later, I received a phone call
while eating dinner at the Village Café in
Lake Tomahawk. It was Donna calling.

"What's going on?"

"Your never going to believe this." She was all excited.

"Believe what?"

"My new coffee pot just unplugged itself. And I know it wasn't you who's doing it."

I chuckled.

"It's not funny!"

"Well, you're never going to guess who I'm having a fish fry with?"

"Who?"

"Jeff Ceason. He came in from Arizona."

"Who's Jeff Ceason?"

"You're not going to believe this, but he's Buckskin's son."

Jimmy Goes High-Tech

Jimmy praying with Franciscan Br. Rodd Umlauf during his last Christian Mass in the back room of the Happy Daze tavern, shortly before Jimmy passed.

I first heard about Jimmy's passing from Jessica Kuhkann, a waitress at the Village Café. As I walked past Happy Daze Tavern, I spotted a small makeshift memorial on a table in front of the main entrance. Jimmy had been ill. When I asked Jessica how he was doing, she told me he had passed away earlier that day. This saddened me. I had seen him less than a week earlier, and he seemed to be in good spirits.

That night, I returned to the Happy Daze parking lot with paranormal equipment, in hopes of observing evidence of unusual activity. Except for a light being left on in the back room where Jimmy had lived out his final days, everything seemed normal. (Anyone who knew Jimmy, knew he didn't leave that light on.)

I ended up missing Jimmy's funeral by a couple of days, so the first chance I got, I went to the Wilderness Rest Cemetery, located a few miles south of town, to pay my last respects. This time, I had a new piece of paranormal gear with me that I was eager to try out.

After finding Jimmy's resting place, I set up my Mel Meter with R.E.M. Pod. I said a few prayers and then started to ask him questions out loud—hoping no one would see me standing there and talking to myself.

"Is there an afterlife?"

"How are you adjusting to it?"

"If there is, can you give me a signal or sign that you are OK?"

I waited some time for a response but nothing happened. I said a parting prayer and returned to my cabin.

Now, anybody who knows me knows I often don't answer my cell phone, or even carry it with me. If I do have it, it's usually not turned on.

I didn't have it with me when I returned to the cabin. The second I entered the cabin door, my phone began to ring. (Turns out, I had placed it on a log next to an outlet—it was charging and on.)

The phone's screen lit up with my wife Donna's name.

As soon as I answered, I heard Donna begin to speak, but the way her voice sounded triggered an old memory.

My mind raced back to when my father passed away. The year was 1997. There was a distorted message left on our landline answering machine at home. The voice was almost mechanical sounding. To this day, I believe it was my deceased father's final message to me.

Back to the present. When Donna said hello, it was in that same distorted, mechanical-sounding voice I heard when my father died. This time, whatever was causing it was transforming Donna's voice. Even in my shocked state, I managed to grab my iPad and start recording. (Check out my

YouTube link, where you can listen and watch this and other recordings.

Question for the reader: *Was this the sign I had asked Jimmy for?*

My cell phone had never done this before or after that trip to the cemetery.

Another thing happened on my cell phone shortly after the phone call from Donna. Unfortunately, somewhere along the line, I lost the video, but did find these still shots.

"Blue Face" on my cellphone while viewing
A YouTube video on Messenger.
Possibly another sign?

Check out the color photos on my FaceBook page (@hauntedlaketomahawk).

I had some of my team members do research on what could cause skin to appear blue like it had on my cell phone. Their research came up empty; there was nothing to be found on the Web about it. But they did concur that it may have been some form of editing, and offered no other explanation.

But who would do such a thing and why? I find it hard to believe that somebody would do this.

One last thought. As I was having these surreal experiences, I felt an all-encompassing presence surrounding me in the cabin.

Note: I have heard reported on different paranormal podcasts that a phenomenon called "blue face" can occur when spirits from the other side try to make contact.

Question to the readers: *Can modern-day electronics (cell phones, computers, iPads, etc.) be a means through which ghosts can manipulate or use to communicate with us?*

GRANNY'S GARAGE

The Long-Awaited Reunion Dance

Please sign into my YouTube channel, https://www.youtube.com/@hauntedlake-tomahawk to view the footage you are about to read about. This event took place on October 9th, 2021.

To me, what was captured demonstrates that some form of our energy, most often referred to as the soul, does indeed exist, and continues on after we have passed from this physical plane of existence. What this continuum, is though, I cannot say, but not only do I believe it exists, it also appears to demonstrate intelligence.

The search for this type of evidence was one of my main motivators for originally writing this book. Little did I know that the proof I was seeking would come from a member of my own family—my mother.

With this, my search has gone full circle and I have for the most part been satisfied to learn that a part of us does indeed survive bodily death.

How long does this continuation last? Again, I cannot say. I do not know if time is even relevant in that state of existence. I did pick up an interesting tidbit from my dad's younger sister, Sr. Theresa SSND, who said, "Your mother told me that she would constantly see your father after he passed away. He never left her side—that went on for 24 years."

Sr. Theresa's words prompted my thinking that time might not exist in this other state. Perhaps each individual is different in this regard, as to the aspect of time and what rate our energy is reabsorbed, or disseminated, back into the universe.

But what if our energy is not totally absorbed? Might these remnants or residuals explain the existence of what we call ghosts? Or might we have options to remain as long as we choose? Are we capable of navigating back and forth or even being in more than one place at a time?

Who's to say? Death may be more complicated than life.

As you can see, there are many more questions, but as far as I'm concerned, at least a small piece of the puzzle was revealed: We do go on.

My mother, Margret Palbicki, passed away on October 6th, 2021 at the age of 93. On October 10th, the family met at her condo around 3:00 p.m. to begin going through some old photos and assemble picture boards for her funeral.

That was when I first viewed the security camera footage. I immediately knew what I was watching. To me, it was a parting gift from my recently deceased mother.

On October 6th, Mom's last day, she was, for the most part, incoherent. Morphine had been administered to ease her of any pain or discomfort.

As I was tending to her, swabbing her mouth to keep it moist, I held her hand and started talking to her. I told her to be brave, and that it was her time to return back home.

"Mom, when you get there, you make sure to say hi to Pa from me, and if it's at all possible, could you please send me some kind of a sign or signal to let me know that you are o.k.?" She suddenly bit down on the swab, which signaled to me that she fully understood what I was saying to her.

That was the last time I would ever speak to my mother.

What the security camera captured in her garage confirmed to me that she was more than o.k., and to date, this is the most compelling piece of evidence I have ever witnessed.

#

I know my emotions were running way too high and that I was way too close to this situation. I needed the assistance of my paranormal investigation team to give me their unbiased and unabated opinions on what the camera had captured the evening of October 9th, 2021.

View the actual footage on my YouTube channel: https://www.YouTube.com/@ HauntedLakeTomahawk. Watch and decide for yourself.

Weather conditions the night of October 9th were as follows:

- 13.9% waxing crescent moon.
- 20 mph wind gusts
- SE direction
- 40% cloud cover.
- Sunset 6:20 PM

I was careful not to intrude on my paranormal team members' opinions in any way, shape, or form. I had them view the video individually, and then asked them write down their thoughts.

Here are their statements/reports/ analyses on what they saw, after viewing the recording.

Fulcrum Team Reports

Scot Mortier

Watching the video (not the entire 1 hour and 20 minutes reported) made me break down the questions into two categories:
1) Equipment used
2) Site stimulus

I. Equipment

- WYZE Cameras, 7 of them
    - What type of sensors are on this model?
    - Infra red?
    - Visible light?
    - Motion detection?

- What are the design specs for each sensor? What are they each designed to capture, and what sets them off?

- Are there known problems with each sensor?
- How do they handle reflections?
- Can a reflection set off the motion detector?

- What sets off the recorder?
  - Can a reflection set off the recorder?
  - How long does the recorder stay active after a sensor sets it off?
  - Do the cameras/sensors share any data between them?

  -

2. Software issues:

- Is an internet connection required or are the cameras hardwired?
- Can the cameras be accessed via the Internet?
  - How fast does the system write recordings? Limits of the speed via the internet connection, signal strength, effect on recordings?

- What kind of media captures the recordings?
- Limits of the media affect on recordings?
- Are there any known software bugs that affect sensors/recording?
- Shape changes, recording pixelization, temperature, humidity, electro-magnetic interference

- Has anyone recorded footage similar to the video?
- How would an expert in photography/ engineering explain causes for the footage?
- How long were the cameras there?
  - 3 to 4 months

II. Site stimulus
- Who had access to the cameras?
- Who had access to the footage?

- Is there a record of who accessed each? (electronically recorded?)
- Can a person with access control any aspects of the camera's/sensor's set the parameters for what sets it off? (sensitivity)
- Set time/date?
- Set the recording speed?
- When did the alarm go off?
- Who responded to it and what happened after that?
- What did they do?
- Who was at the site when the alarm went off?
- If nobody was there, unable to report the surrounding circumstances in the immediate vicinity?
- Can find the moon phase? (reflection questions)
- Can find neighborhood spinners? (garden decorations)

- Can find if official vehicle (squad, ambulance, fire truck) was in the vicinity with lights going?
- What else would explain the what's on camera?
  - Mice?
  - Birds?
  - Spider webs?
  - Bugs?
  - Lights inside/outside?
  - Reflecting surfaces inside/outside?
  - Light chains?
  - Motion sources inside/outside?

- Reported to the author (after viewing)
  - Reporter's mother had passed 3 days prior.
  - Sister with access to video footage reports alarm went off on garage camera
  - 1 hour 20 minutes of 'orb' footage

Analysis:

- Googling orb footage results in many videos of orbs captured
- The orbs captured in this case do not appear to be caused by spiderwebs, bugs
- I say that because of the movement as compared to those other causes, my experience as a photographer, and previous recordings and explanations reviewed/ observed.
- This video shows 2 orbs that split into 4 occasionally.
- When they split into 4, they dim.
- Their movement is coordinated (not in different directions)
- There are moments of pixelization
- It is unknown if the orbs are being recorded in infra red or visible The pixelizations are a common occurrence for digital devices and recorders. I find it insignificant for that reason.

- The orbs appear to be a reflection off a surface that was moving.
  - Unknown if it was inside or outside the garage.
  - It had somewhat of a pattern that repeated, then purportedly stopped at one point.
- It is unknown if the alarm was set off more than once that night.
- It is unknown if there have been any other alarms since cameras installed.
- A reflection off a moving surface is the most likely explanation of the footage in my opinion.
- It is unknown what the surface would be or what light source would be reflecting off of it.

Because I was never on site, only viewed most of the video, I cannot eliminate or add anything additional at this time.

The summary is really still my final process of elimination:
1) not a spider web
2) not insects

Likely reflections picked up by the cameras sensors/software.

Light source could be from outside or inside the garage, really difficult to tell.

Pixelization is just that: pixelization. That's most likely related to interference in the WIFI signal or based on the read/write speed of the media that stored the footage.

Additionally, without more data from the camera company's design and program engineers, explaining what types of sensors are incorporated into this surveillance camera, and what those sensor are designed to notice, and/or known glitches with the sensors and software, the issue will remain unsubstantiated.

My conclusion remains that this is unsubstantiated as a supernatural phenomena.

Jeff Braun

I was given the opportunity to view a security video that was recorded in the garage of Margaret Palbicki a few days after her passing.

The WYZE camera is activated by motion.

What I saw were bright circular orbs moving all about in the garage area. Sometimes two orbs moved together, sometimes three or four. They seemed to move intelligently and in unison.

This phenomenon continued for several minutes. Back and forth, up and down. The video ended when the orbs moved quickly to the right and off screen.

The experience was remarkable to me because the camera had not recorded any such event in the past or since.

Also eerie is the fact that during her last days, Mark had asked his mother to send him a sign that she was all right.

No evidence has come forth to explain the phenomena.

Pat Barney

My take on the video from Mark's mother's garage

Watching the video, there does not appear to be any direct light hitting the camera lens, nor is it likely that indirect/reflected lighting was the cause. The garage lights were out, and it appears that no light was coming in from the windows. The only light source available is the camera's IR LEDs.

The moving light orbs do not appear to be an optical distortion caused by the lens or some digital glitch in the playback.

I believe what is seen in the video was a spiderweb moving back an forth in front of the camera. The multiple light "orbs" seen are possibly multiple spokes of the web coming into camera view. A very light draft would be enough to cause the web to sway back and forth out of the camera's frame. The camera's IR LEDs may have accentuated the web. This seems plausible after reading comments in the Wyze camera forum, where people reported similar unusual sightings only to find a cobweb.

Br. Rodd Umlauf

My first impressions are the strongest thoughts generated from this home security video. There are two strong orbs of light that move in a synchronized, harmonious, flowing, and flying motion. The closeness and perfect harmony reminded me of a couple experienced in ball-room dance and lovers of each other, as they float in a gliding dance across the room, as if there were a mystical music band playing in the background. I could see this couple of souls truly dancing and loving the night away in perfect unison with the band.

When the two orbs of light divided into three, and then four, I was set back in my thought. Then they united again into two "dancing" images of light. That was confusing to my first thoughts.

Another thought that crossed my mind is that I have seen supposed "UFO" videos of light orbs in the sky which move in unison.

This security video is truly a puzzle to me but it is fun to imagine that a couple once separated by life and death have now been reunited in the intermediate state before the resurrections of the Body on the Last Day to enjoy each others close dance embrace.

Author and Team Fulcrum's Leader's Report, Mark Palbicki

This is what I saw in my heart of hearts. My eyes were transfixed to what I was watching.

Orbs seemed to appear from the wall just in front of the door, at first one , two, three, and finally four.

Their movement seemed synchronized, and were more flow-like as they moved in unison. It didn't take long for me to recognize that what I was watching was a dance.

They were dancing.

OMG! It's Mom and Dad! They're having their long-awaited reunion dance.

This continued for almost one hour and twenty minutes.

What intrigued me the most is when the infrared camera tried to pixelate the form(s) it was trying to pick up.

At that point, I froze the video and took stills, every second or split second. What I found astounded me.

First off, it differentiated the orbs as separate, and not just one single orb being reflected .

Then it appeared that the camera was trying to make out what appears to be two individual shapes that formed into transparent bodies. That, to me, did indeed look like a couple dancing. I took the liberty to outline the shapes of what I believe I saw, but also included the originals so you can compare and decide for yourself.

There was also missing time. One second of time disappeared during the duration of the pixelation. The second cannot be accounted for.

Then, at the end, the orbs changed into smaller shapes as they re-entered the wall from which they had come. We'll let the evidence speak for itself, and you can decide.

I can and will say that for the last six months of my mother's life, we had cared for her in a home hospice situation. Toward the end of her life, she would talk and hold conversations to deceased loved ones, especially her late husband George (my father), as if he were sitting right next to you on the couch, or standing off in a corner at a distance.

All family care providers and nursing staff reported the same or similar phenomenon. She even saw her beloved pet dog, Fluffy, and she would bend down from her reclining chair as if to call Fluffy with a treat in her hand.

Could what my mother had been experiencing possibly be related to the phrase "your life passes before your very eyes."? Could she have been reliving memories in her mind?

I tried multiple times to capture some sort of evidence with my Mel and EMF meters during this time frame, but to no avail. As I am writing now, it dawned on me that perhaps an EVP recorder would have been a wiser choice of paranormal equipment to use.

Author's conclusion:

You can tell from my own team's observations and conclusions that no matter how overwhelming the evidence may appear to one person, it might not necessarily appear like that to another. This is the conundrum in which we find ourselves in on a daily basis navigating through life.

Images from
Granny's Garage

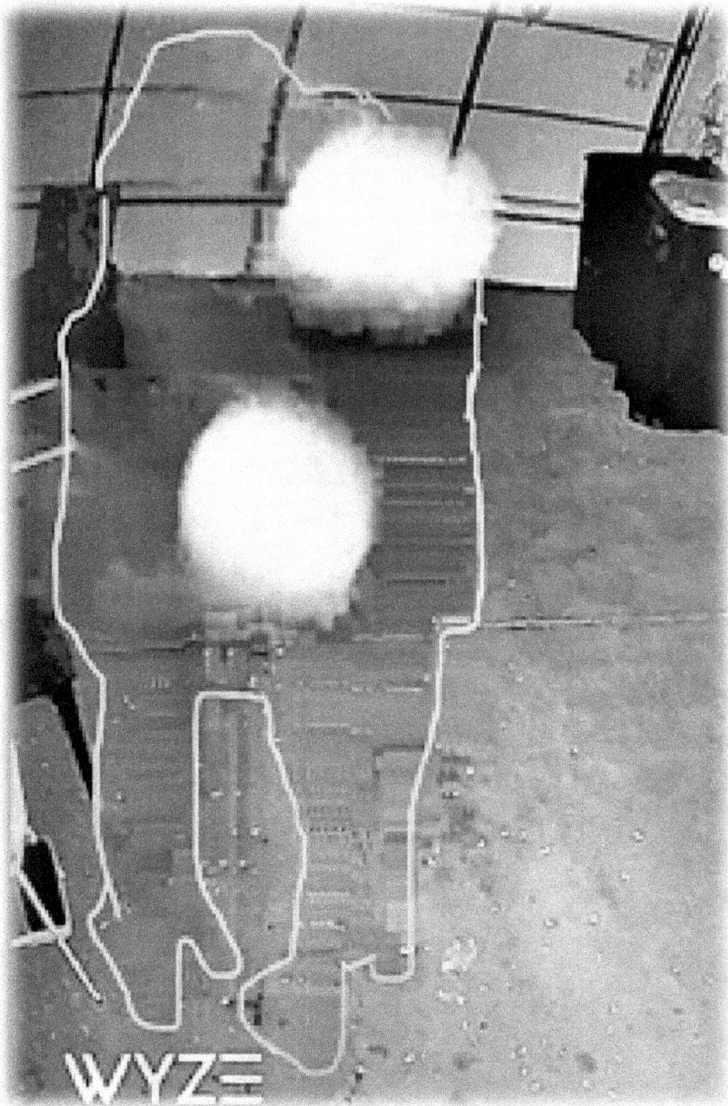

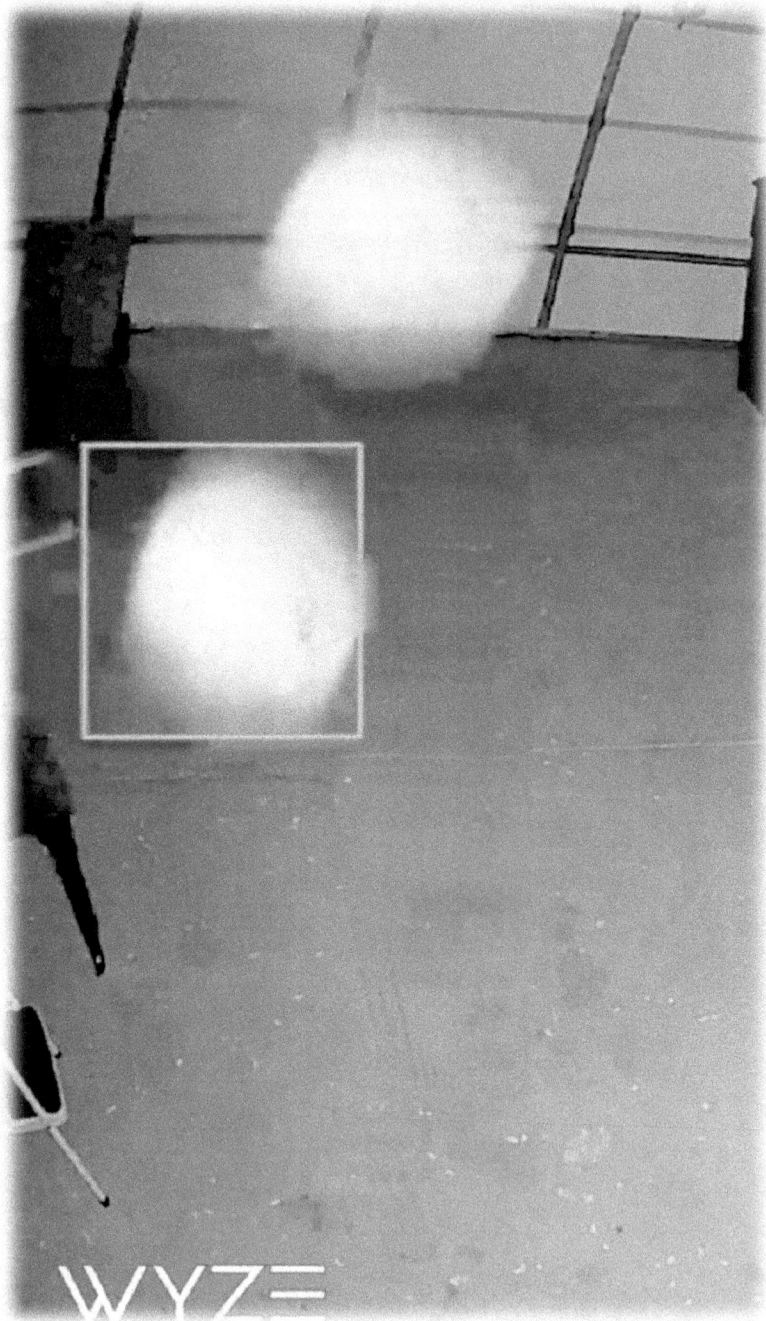

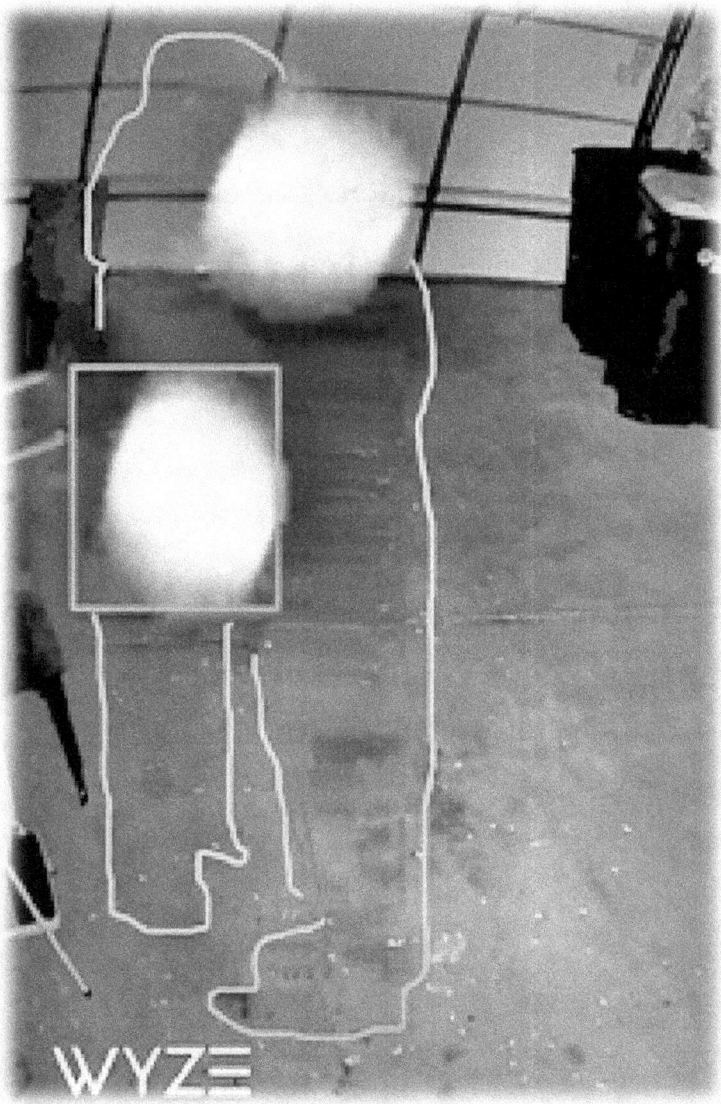

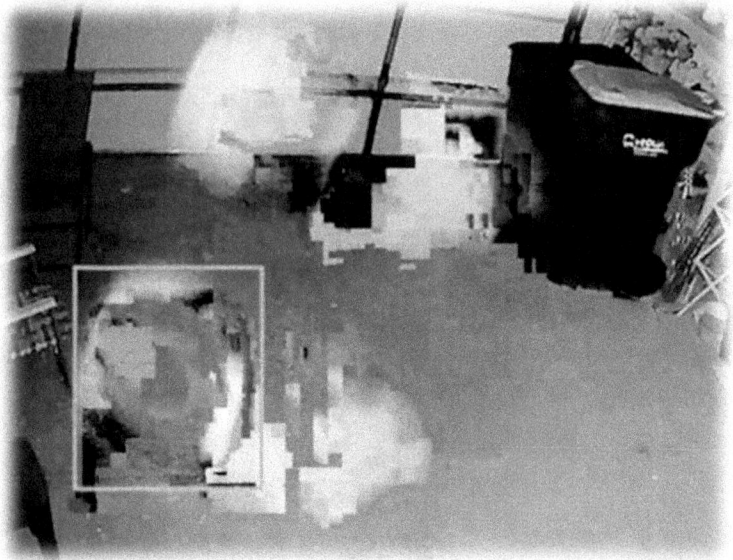

In the author's opinion, the above still photo appears to be a view from top looking down, from the tops of their heads. Notice the similar hairstyle.

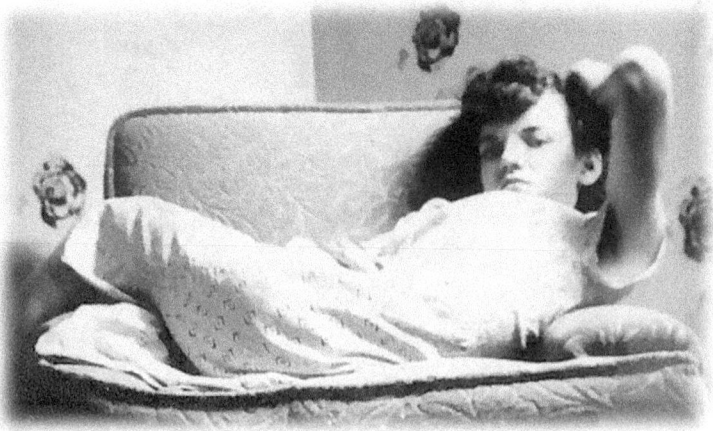

Young Margret Palbicki

The image above was generated by the Smart Edge function in 2022 edition of Corel's Paintshop Pro 64 bit.

EQUIPMENT

One of the author's prized possessions is famed ghosthunter Hereward Carrington's radiomicrometer

We are living in exciting times, especially for us ghost hunters!

The main reason for this is the high level of technology that has become available to us, and without breaking the bank. It wasn't that long ago when we didn't have the internet, GPS, cell phones, and other highly sophisticated pieces of equipment. Now we have more information at our fingertips than in any other time in man's known history, those of us ghost hunting included. I could carry on about today's technology but I won't. There are other books written about it.

But if you're anything like me, you're having a hard time keeping up with the fast-paced and ever-changing tech world that we live in. So let's just say that like me, you may not have the latest and or greatest tech that's out there, I know I don't.

Here are my two cents' worth: "It's what you do with what you have." Having the latest, up-to-date equipment or the most expensive equipment is all fine, but it doesn't necessarily make you a good ghost hunter. Learn to make do with what you have, learn to follow or trust your gut feelings, your intuition, and it's with the combination of your natural abilities and the aid of modern-day technology that you may very well have some kind of breakthrough in the field of ghost hunting.

Recommended readings: *Strange Frequencies (A Practical Guide to Paranormal Technology)* by Craig Telesha and *Armor of God (Prayers for Protection and Deliverance)* by Dave Juliano.

Protection

As I stated earlier, and for the most part, I have only investigated people I knew and were good with in life. Still, I took precautionary measures to ensure the safety of my team. This included prayers and incense, and even the added insurance of Franciscan Friar—now Catholic deacon— Br. Rodd Umlauf.

Br. Rodd Umlauf

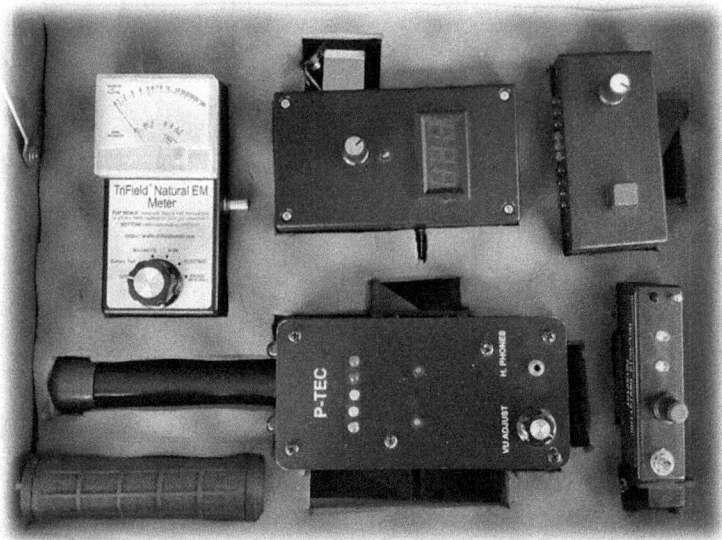

- Upper left: Trifield Natural EM Meter
  Lower center: P-TEC EMF Meter
- Lower right: Nethertech Hot/Cold Deviation Detector
- Upper center: EMF Pump adjustable
- Upper right: Seismograph

- Upper left: Mel Meter MEL-REM-ATDD
- Upper right: Ghost Ware Pro SHADOW PRO V
- Lower left: EDI Multi Meter
- Lower right: Dual Sweep Frequency ITC
- Research Device: P-SB11

- Upper left: Panasonic RR-QR200 EVP Recorder
- Lower left: DAS Crosshair Thermal Detector
- Upper center: Infrared Thermometer
- Middle left: ITC P-SB7 Spirit Box with speaker
- Right side: Catch a Ghost Yes/No analyzer

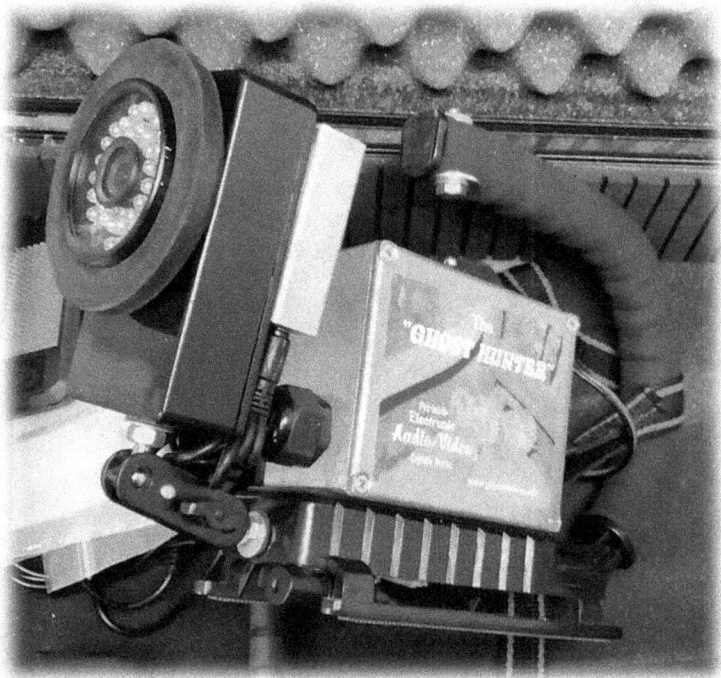

♦ The Ghost Hunter portable electronic audio/
video capture device

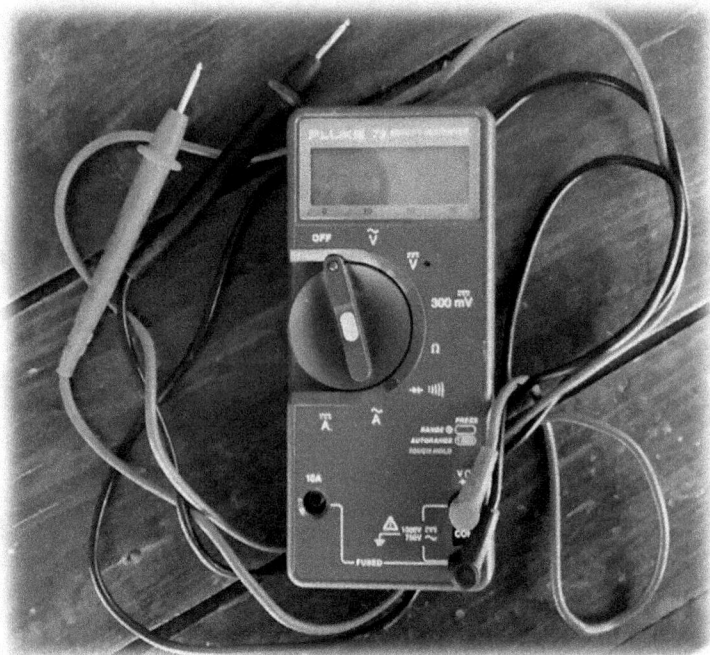

♦ Fluke 73 series II multimeter

♦ Left: Hand-held HT-175 Thermal Imaging camera, 32x32 resolution
♦ Right: Nest Cam

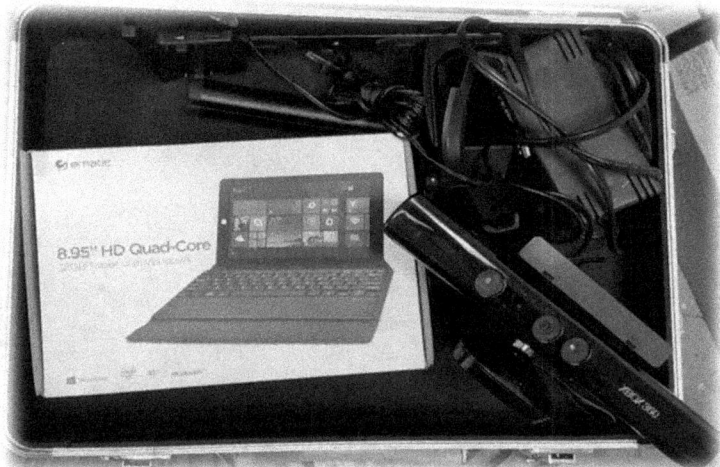

♦ Kinect Camera produces stick figure images

♦ D.J. Button's Portal Response Box

Author sitting in a crop circle near
Mayville, Wisconsin (2003).

AUTHOR'S COMMENTS

Hi, Mark Palbicki here. This is my first attempt at writing a book, so please have patience with my wording and sentence structure. I never received higher than a letter grade of C in any of my English classes, and I still type one finger at a time. This book endeavor has been a real challenge, but one I needed to help overcome my cancer diagnosis.

With that out of the way, I have been traveling to Lake Tomahawk and the surrounding areas in northern Wisconsin for more than 25 years. I have been interested in the paranormal for a majority of my adult life. For the most part, it started after an accident in which I was struck by a car, back in 1977. This resulted in what nowadays is known as a ***near-death experience*** (NDE) in the form of an ***out-of-body experience*** (OBE).

The accident and those injuries proved to be a life changing event, resulting in my constant pursuit of knowledge pertaining to the paranormal including, NDEs, ghosts, afterlife survival, quantum physics, OBEs, reincarnation, and really just about anything I could get my hands on at that time that might explain what happened to me.

It wasn't until my wife's second pregnancy with our daughter Katelyn that my belief system started to change. I was born and raised as a Roman Catholic, and was taught not to believe in such nonsense as reincarnation, only to discover that the more I read and studied on the subject, the more questions I had—questions that my faith could not answer.

So began a great conflict within myself, a battle that lasted about ten years, during which I suffered a bout of deep depression. It finally ended with a paradigm shift in my belief system.

My resolve was to make this world a better place in which to live, by proving that an afterlife did indeed exist, with or without religion. I often questioned myself, what would the world be like if we actually lived our lives with purpose and reasoned in a good, moral type of way, and what if, our time here on earth really did matter?

Just think of all the advancements mankind could make if we only learned to row this vessel we call Earth in the same direction (instead of in circles).

I believe that uncovering evidence of an afterlife could make a difference. Even if my research only reaches one person who'd rethink his or her thoughts and actions in a positive way, my time writing this book would be well spent.

Now, nothing against any of the world's organized religions or their members. If that's what grounds you and makes you whole, more power to you. It's just not the direction I follow any more. And for my atheist friends out there who wish to believe that they are worm food after this existence, who am I to say that you're not? Good luck with that.

Sorry, but my ego simply isn't big enough that it can fool me into thinking I know everything there is to know about this unfathomable mystery into which we have been born.

If you want to talk about supernatural or paranormal beings, I reason that Jesus Christ has got to be on top, or near the top of everyone's list. So, as you can tell, I no longer find myself a *religious* person, but do consider myself a *spiritual* being.

I do believe in Love, and that God is Love. I consider myself a sensitive, having some psychic and/or clairvoyant abilities. I willfully confess that I have no real control over when and why these abilities will come into play, but they do help me from time to time as I navigate my way through this world by recognizing life's little signs and signals. My clairvoyant experiences mostly come in the form of precognitive dreams.

I like to draw a comparison of being psychically gifted to that of a talent, like an artist, musician, author, or athlete. Take the talent required to be a musician, for example. There are a few rare, truly gifted musicians who are born this way. Perhaps they can't even read music, yet the music just comes out of them naturally. They are the true geniuses in their field. Savants may very well be a prime example of this general theory.

Other musicians, who possess raw talent, will practice until their fingers bleed, have abilities that grow until they become second nature, like muscle memory. Most of us will never truly possess this musical gift, no matter how great our desires are.

I think the same thing rings true with psychic abilities. I believe that all humans possess some level of psychic ability; it's in our nature. But like a talent, it depends on what end of the spectrum you fall into. In the right environment, it can be nurtured and built upon, in order to heighten our awareness levels of enlightenment. There are also the very rare, true psychics who are born with their gifts.

Fair warning: I recognize there are also the tricksters, hustling the vulnerable to make a buck. Be careful in your own personal search.

I also believe it is possible that psychic abilities can be inherited, possibly even skipping a generation before reappearing. Some of my mother's siblings are said to have possessed this gift of insightful dreaming.

One question I have for my readers is: Could there be an imprint on one's DNA, like a genetic memory? Maybe this is what we call "instinct"—birds knowing how to build nests, beavers knowing how to build dams, the migration patterns of animals.

I believe there's also another way, that can find your inner psychic talent—by having a Near-Death Experience (NDE).

I have been involved in NDE studies with Dr. Bruce Greyson at the University of Virginia for the past 25 plus years on this phenomenon. I think trauma plays a major contributing role in expanding psychic abilities.

As far as I can figure, both the psychic gifts from my mother's side of the family and having experienced an NDE helped contribute to me being who I am. I hope this makes you think, and I hope you enjoy the book.

Mark

CONCLUSION

I'm not here to convince you of the existence of ghosts. That, you must decide for yourself.

Each of us perceives the world differently, as only we can, through our own eyes. However, how our vision is shaped varies in different ways; be it through religion, education, culture, experience, economics, or superstition, we all view life through our personal filters.

So, believe what you will; it's your own belief system, and I'm good with that.

There is no right or wrong here—there just is.

What I do know is that we all share the common bond called death. Regardless of what you believe in, the fact is that some day, we are all going to die. That is a tough topic of discussion which most people don't like to talk about.

You might call it a silly superstition, but in all walks of life, and to all degrees of intelligence, ghosts are a worldwide phenomenon. Reports of them are not going away anytime soon.

Think for yourself and draw your own conclusions.

One final note to readers:

I've been ostracized by some and told I'm going to hell by others, for participating in the activities explained here and writing this book. You should know there was no nefarious intent in the making of it. I only hope this contribution on the subject will help solve a small piece of the puzzle of the, as of now, unfathomable mystery into which we where born.

Thanks for reading
Mark

Mark Palbicki

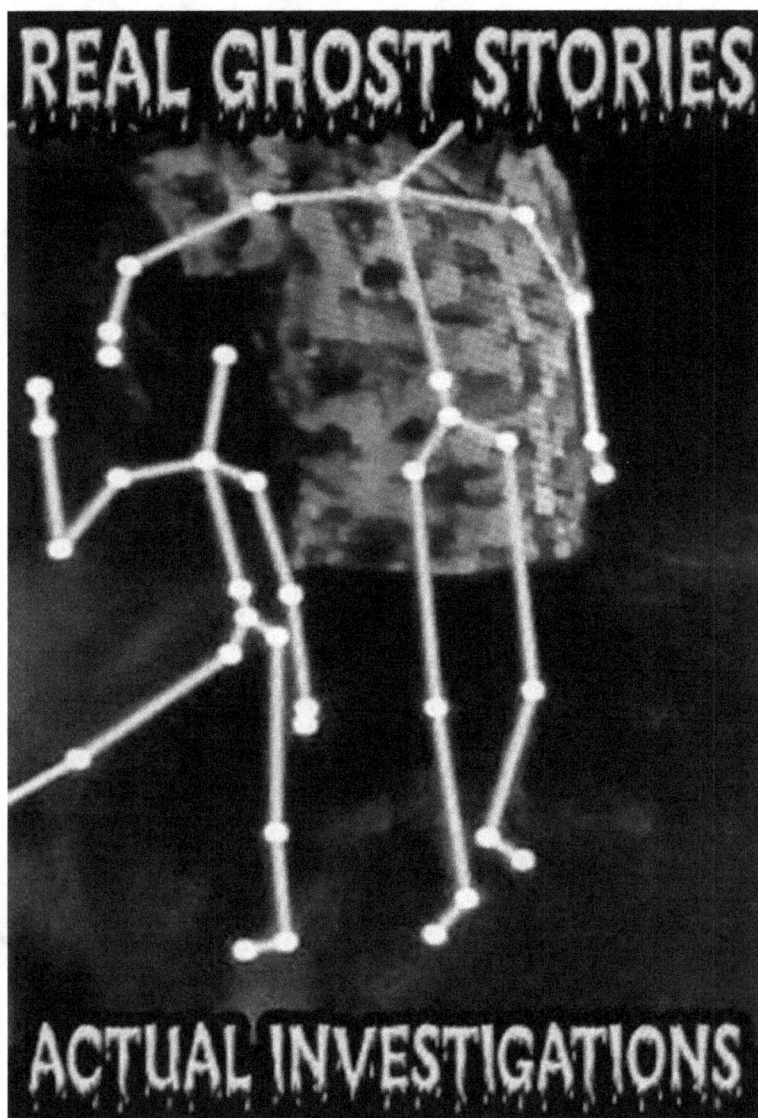

HAUNTED LAKE TOMAHAWK

www.ingramcontent.com/pod-product-compliance
Lightning Source LLC
Chambersburg PA
CBHW062157270326
41930CB00009B/1568